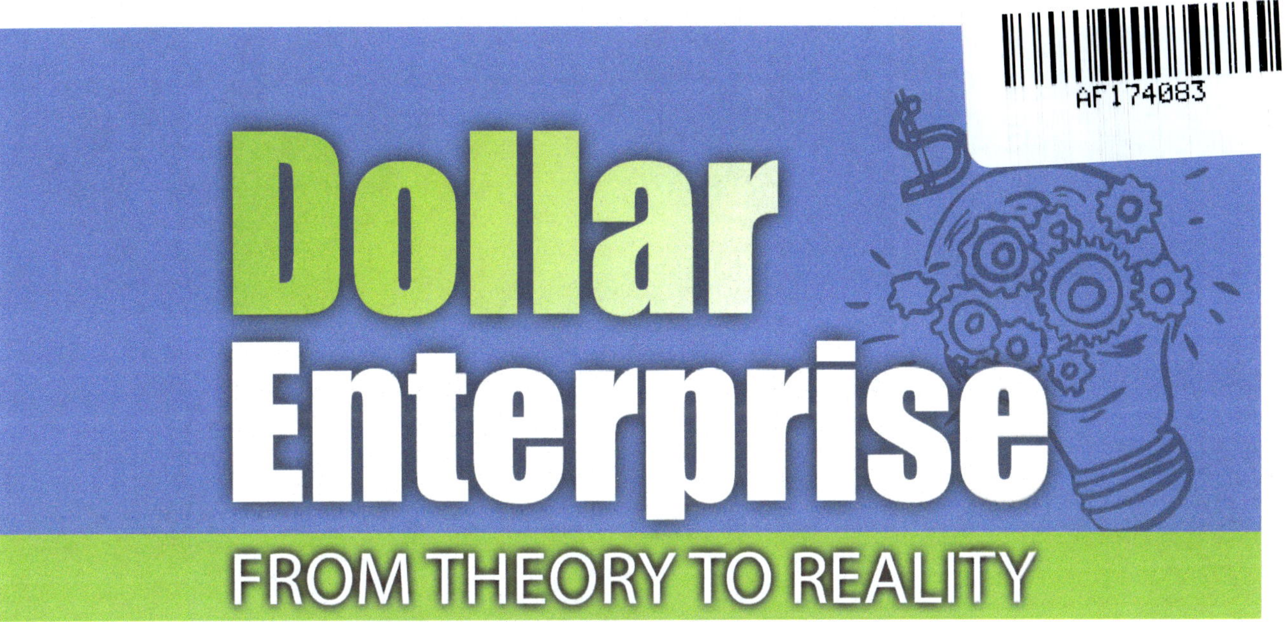

Dollar Enterprise

FROM THEORY TO REALITY

An Experimental Learning Exercise Applying Community Entrepreneurship To Plan & Operate A Small Venture on Campus

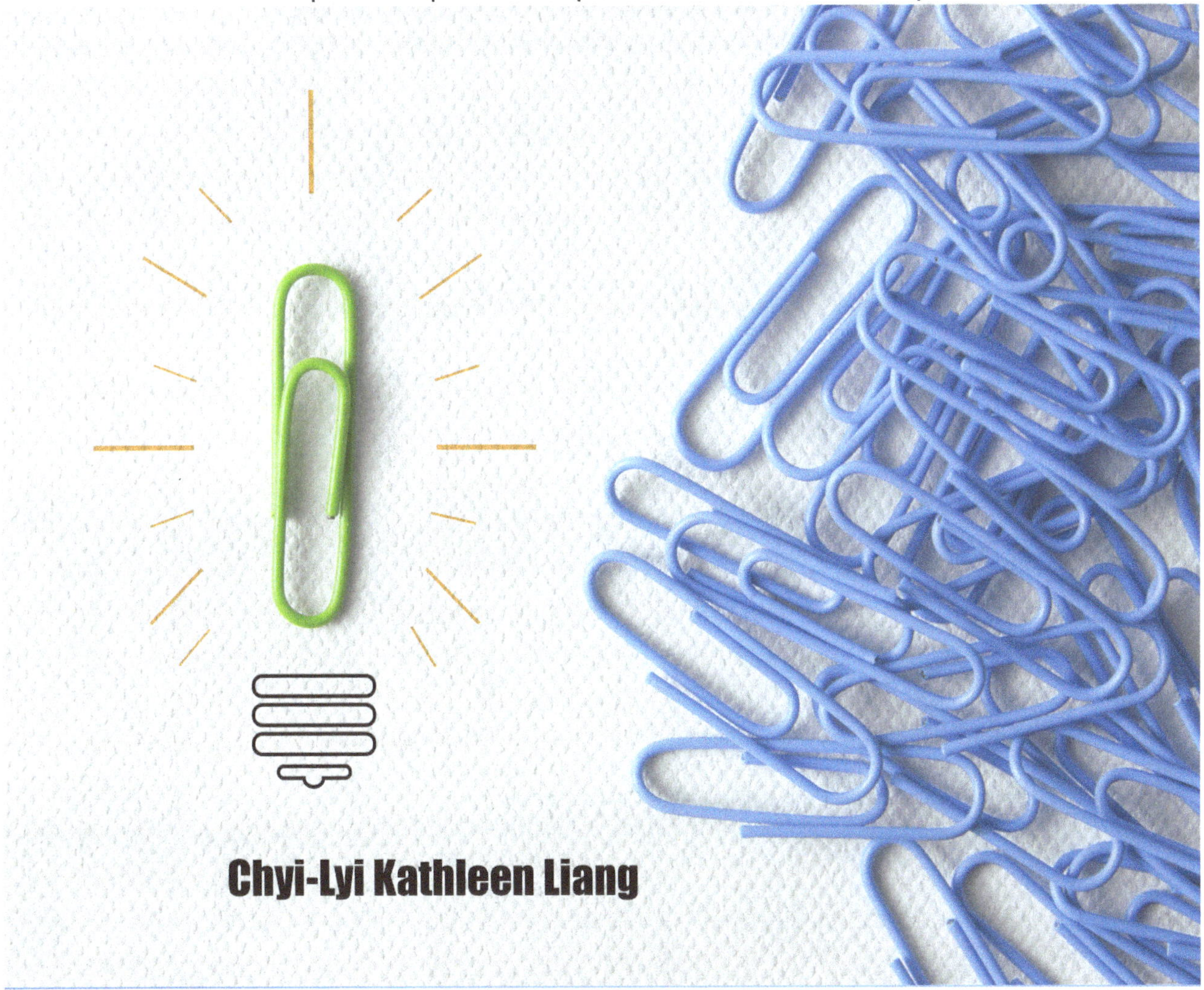

Chyi-Lyi Kathleen Liang

Kendall Hunt
publishing company

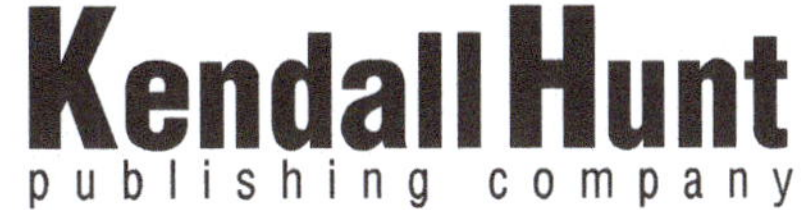

Cover images: © Shutterstock.com and also Courtesy of Chyi-Lyi (Kathleen) Liang

Kendall Hunt
publishing company

www.kendallhunt.com
Send all inquiries to:
4050 Westmark Drive
Dubuque, IA 52004-1840

TABLE OF CONTENTS

Chyi-Lyi (Kathleen) Liang, PhD

W. K. Kellogg Distinguished Professor of Sustainable Agriculture
Director, Center for Environmental Farming Systems

- PhD 1996 Purdue University   Agricultural Economics
- MS 1991 Purdue University   Agricultural Economics
- BS 1987 National Taiwan University   Agricultural Economics

Areas of Expertise
Community and social entrepreneurship, food systems/networks, applied economics, econometrics, environmental economics, tourism

Contact Information
North Carolina Agricultural & Technical State University
College of Agriculture and Environmental Sciences
Coltrane Hall, Room 105-B
1601 East Market Street
Greensboro, NC 27411

Office 336 285 4683   Fax 336 334 7432
cliang@ncat.edu

Dr. Liang is an award-winning educator who has designed, developed, and implemented innovative courses in entrepreneurship to incorporate service-learning and experiential learning. Her research, teaching, and outreach focus on many perspectives of entrepreneurship and its interactions with people, communities, and organizations. Her learn-in-the-now approach to teaching and dynamic interactions with students push them from the classroom into real-life applications. Dr. Liang has taught over 6,000 students at all levels (K-12, college, post college, and non-conventional learners), advised numerous new ventures in the United States, and served in leadership positions in more than 20 national and international organizations. She has received more than $6 million grants from the U.S. Department of Agriculture and other organizations to conduct innovative projects to explore, examine, assess, and analyze situations with respect to food and farming systems, multifunctional strategies, and rural development. She has published and presented numerous peer reviewed articles relating to multifunctional agriculture, entrepreneurship, and regional food systems/networks.

Who would believe $1 seed money can create miracles? It has been over 10 years since I created Dollar Enterprise at the University of Vermont. When I started my position at the University of Vermont in 1998 as a new Assistant Professor, my primary responsibility was to design, create, and sustain a program to replace an old agri-business curriculum. Not only this new program had to work well and fit well in the mission of College of Agriculture and Life Sciences, there was a strong expectation for this program to receive national and international recognitions in the long term. It was a very challenging task for a new Assistant Professor!

I really appreciate all the support from my colleagues at University of Vermont and other institutions who are willing to entertain such a crazy idea. I remember when I presented the concept of Dollar Enterprise to my Department Chair and the Dean in 2005, their first question was: "Why is it so important for you to do this?" My answer: "The only way I know how to teach entrepreneurship, is to let students learn through action, experience, and living in the moment while they test entrepreneurship theories." My dream became true when University of Vermont administrators agreed to give me a chance, which was a very brave and risky decision. If it worked, this program would be the first one in the United States to teach entrepreneurship and community development through integration of theories, experiential learning, and service learning in the Colleges of Agriculture. If it did not work, well, we tried. Now after more than 10 years, Dollar Enterprise is still standing strong at the University of Vermont. I have shared stories, strategies, process, and learning assessment of Dollar Enterprise in numerous presentations and workshops.

Since August 1, 2016, I joined the College of Agriculture and Environmental Sciences at the North Carolina Agricultural and Technical State University. It is really exciting for me to establish Dollar Enterprise as a new course in a new institution, and I will offer the first class of Dollar Enterprise in Fall 2017.

As an educator, the most exciting thing for me is to see sparks in students' eyes. When each person walks into my classroom the first day, no one has any idea what this class is about. No one could foresee, not even me, how challenging Dollar Enterprise would be. No matter how much I prepare students, there are always surprises every day. Here are some classic memorable moments from different years:

For example,

1. Someone dumped coffee ground in the sink of library bathroom, and created flooding situation.
2. It is supposed to be common sense that we don't wash bright color clothes with white T-shirts.
3. Counting money and complete daily financial records are nightmares!
4. Someone actually robbed a Dollar Enterprise team member in front of library!
5. Our teams accidentally tripped the electricity outlets in library—we are out of power in library for a few hours.
6. No one seems to pay attention about apple cider issues—we are not supposed to re-heat apply cider!
7. I have to teach students the correct way to do dishes, wash produce, and cook food using creative recipe.

8. We constantly receive warnings from staff members about Dollar Enterprise teams removing tables and chairs from other locations.

9. The storage room could be messy from time to time—students needed to learn how to organize storage space to accommodate 11–13 teams at the same time.

How do I know learning has occurred? Comments posted on Facebook discussion groups often show clear information about communication strategies, team scheduling, human resource management, inventory management, pricing strategies, inventory control, and cost structure:

For example, teams used Facebook to communicate shopping trips, reporting on inventory shortage, arranging cooking and food delivery services, members responding to tabling issues and lack of coordinated efforts to share responsibilities, team members calculating unit cost versus pricing strategies (are we using too much cheese on one sandwich), and how to deal with leftover inventories.

Discussions of quality control were often critical for teams. Team members had shared Information about which type of bread was more popular among customers. Team members posted video teaching each other to use credit card machine, to count money correctly, and to deposit money correctly. Team members also communicated about workload, time management, and conflicts against certain issues or members. One of the most impressive outcomes of Dollar Enterprise was to experience how each team solved their own problems from time to time. If they had issues with certain members, we would call a *platform meeting* in class time, inviting teams to come up to the platform and discuss their concerns in public. This strategy helped each team to sit down together, and let each person share thoughts equally. Other teams often provide support and assistance, too, by not being directly involved in private issues.

There are so many more stories for me to share. I thoroughly enjoy creating and implementing Dollar Enterprise, and look forward to many more years to come. I hope this book offers sufficient information and contents to support other educators and trainers to build your own programs—and to have a lot of FUN!

DOLLAR ENTERPRISE—SUMMARY OF DESIGN, IMPLEMENTATION, AND IMPACTS

The mission of Dollar Enterprise is to support the landscape of entrepreneurial learning by offering education and training opportunities for aspiring and nascent entrepreneurs across demographics, learning style, and learning ability to develop three aspects of entrepreneurship that are often omitted in traditional business education and textbooks:

- **Entrepreneurial individuals** through developing mindset, traits, professionalism, ethic, leadership, and creativity using hands-on activities and participatory approach.
- **Entrepreneurial knowledge and skills** through developing communication, team building, business practices, and decision making using group projects and working with community partners focusing on problem solving.
- **Entrepreneurial opportunities** through developing resources, capacity, and networks by working with local organizations, businesses, government agencies, trade associations, and service providers.

The purpose of Dollar Enterprise is to provide an entrepreneurship course for students to learn theories as well as engage in real process of being an entrepreneur simultaneously.

The idea of Dollar Enterprise was created in 2005, the night before the first day of class in Fall semester of 2005 by instructor, Dr. Kathleen Liang. All Dollar Enterprise activities were designed, created, managed, and monitored by the instructor, who also supplied the seed money of $1 to each individual. A team consists of 8–10 individuals and will have $8–$10 per team as seed money. Dollar Enterprise simulates a formation of any business in the real world from building teamwork, identifying and generating resources, creating products, establishing coalitions, supporting community partners, to dealing with day-to-day operations, assessment, optimization, and time management.

This course runs twice a year in each semester. The instructor needs to acquire campus dining service permit to serve food items on campus at least one semester prior to Dollar Enterprise activities. The instructor also needs to reserve venture locations around campus one semester prior to Dollar Enterprise activities. These locations can be outside library, inside/outside student center, and on the greens of campus. Sometimes mobile selling strategies could achieve better goals than having a station. Once the semester begins, it takes one month to prepare student teams and apply for realistic food permits. The contents of business planning and strategies for new venture creation must be covered prior to launching Dollar Enterprise activities. Once teams are engaged in Dollar Enterprise activities, instructors need to continue teaching marketing, management, operation, financial analysis, and risk analysis based on day-to-day issues and challenges. It is essential for instructors to collaborate with teams and offer support to respond to daily issues and challenges particularly when teams encounter communication problems.

Each team runs their business for 4 weeks (at least 3 hours every day from Monday through Friday, between 8 a.m. to 5 p.m.) during each semester in various pre-reserved locations on campus only. At the end of the Dollar Enterprise activities, all proceeds are donated to charity organizations identified by each team.

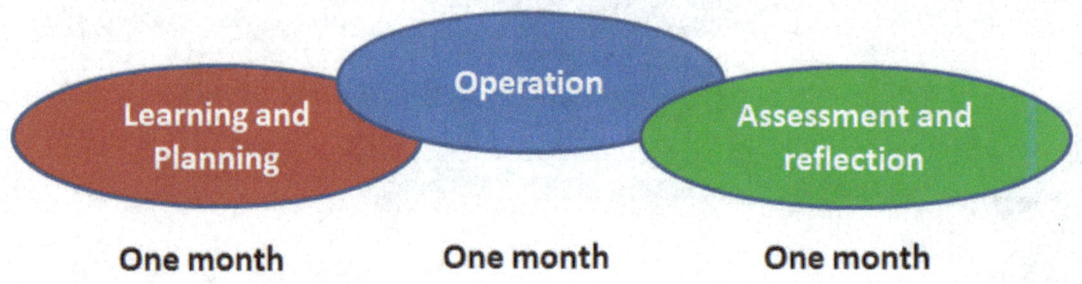

Courtesy of Chyi-lyi (Kathleen) Liang

Each team goes through the same process that any entrepreneur would in creating a new venture—brainstorm ideas, design and create products or services using very limited resource, develop a team policy, organize business structure, assign workload to employees, gather resources (locally sourced ingredients, recycled and reusable materials, and other supplies), conduct market research, define target market and advertising strategies, develop a business plan, develop financial recording systems, conduct financial analysis, assess daily operations, and be prepared to respond to daily unexpected issues.

Weekly team reports and team member's assessments are completed and returned to the instructor at the end of each week throughout the semester, including preparation and planning period, operation period, and concluding period. At the end of the 4-week business operation, each team concludes with a business report, financial report, self-assessment, and final team member assessment. Each team donates all proceeds to local charities.

For Students

Many people are interested in learning about new venture creation, business planning, and entrepreneurship. There are many good references available (for example, United States Small Business Administration, https://www.sba.gov/). This Dollar Enterprise book clearly describes very simple step-by-step procedures for any person who is interested in creating their own venture opportunities in for-profit, not-for-profit, or public service aspects. Different from other business planning materials, this book offers an innovative guide for entrepreneurs-want-to-be utilizing existing, very limited resources to engage in entrepreneurial stages. In real life, most successful entrepreneurs start with very limited resources.

Each learner needs to read each section before lectures to understand:

1. University (or any other institution) policies, regulations, and Code of Conducts.
2. What each step is about, how each step links together, and why each step is important.
3. How to build up the new venture creation process one step at a time.
4. How to link each section's information in creating a business plan.
5. Specific requirement and information needed to be gathered by instructor and students each week and each day.
6. How to create your own products, plan, and communication strategies following samples of good practices (and what not to do).

This book is designed as a guidebook to help each person acquire sufficient information to experience entrepreneurship – what it is, why people become entrepreneurs, how people become entrepreneurs through success and failure, and self-assessment of entrepreneurial characteristics and opportunities.

This book also serves as a workbook, where you can find all assignments and examples. It is the instructor's duty to lead each learner through the process, individually and as a team.

For Teachers

The target audience of Dollar Enterprise is people who are interested in or curious about creating their own opportunities, but have no experience or very limited experience in business planning.

You will find theory of community entrepreneurship, pedagogy of integrated experiential learning and service learning in teaching entrepreneurship, and easy-to-follow instructions to establish Dollar Enterprise procedures or to design your own course in teaching entrepreneurship combing theories and practices.

Entrepreneurship has strong impacts in creating wealth and opportunities. Educators can use this book to motivate and inspire learners to understand what entrepreneurship is about through a process to:

- Create Ideas and Concepts
- Create Products and Services
- Create Knowledge and Skills
- Create Information and Competitive Advantage
- Create Opportunities and Wealth

Most of the educators/teachers received education focusing on conventional disciplines, such as economics, accounting, engineering, or history. When we received our terminal degrees, we became certified subject matter experts, and many subject matter experts became teachers. Most of us have very limited experiences in designing, developing, testing, and implementing teaching pedagogy when we were students. We were taught to learn and to test well, and such mindset seemed to be transferred to young generations who took our classes. Unfortunately, the learning reactions occurred in classrooms may not prepare students well when they have to deal with real life situations, particularly when people have to respond to risks and failure. In an entrepreneur's perspective, finding solutions to handle risks and failures is almost a daily routine. So the question is – Can we actually teach entrepreneurship? And how do we prepare people to become successful entrepreneurs?

To create a successful entrepreneurship program, it will be essential to create entrepreneurial educators first. Building on our knowledge and skills as subject matter specialists, we already have a solid foundation to support learners to obtain contexts and guide learners to use the contexts in problem solving. Educators need to seek opportunities to be creative and innovative through interdisciplinary and multidisciplinary collaborations which will stimulate ideas across conventional fields. There are many training opportunities and resources to support educators to "think outside the box." These training sessions might force us to step out of our comfort zone to engage in conversations, discussions, or exercises that are unfamiliar to us. However, these unconventional interactions should trigger our curiosity to explore, discover, and disseminate new opportunities to engage and motivate our own students.

Before we dive into teaching entrepreneurship, we need to ask and respond to a few questions:

- Am I an entrepreneur?
- Do I have entrepreneurial characteristics to support others?
- Do I have the information, knowledge, and skills to design and implement an effective entrepreneurship course?

Entrepreneurship is not a stand-alone subject like conventional fields. Entrepreneurship is a combination of wisdom, spirit, and life style. It can be covered in any discipline under any condition given any resources (or with no resources). This book will share step-by-step guidance for educators to create your own course with/without resources.

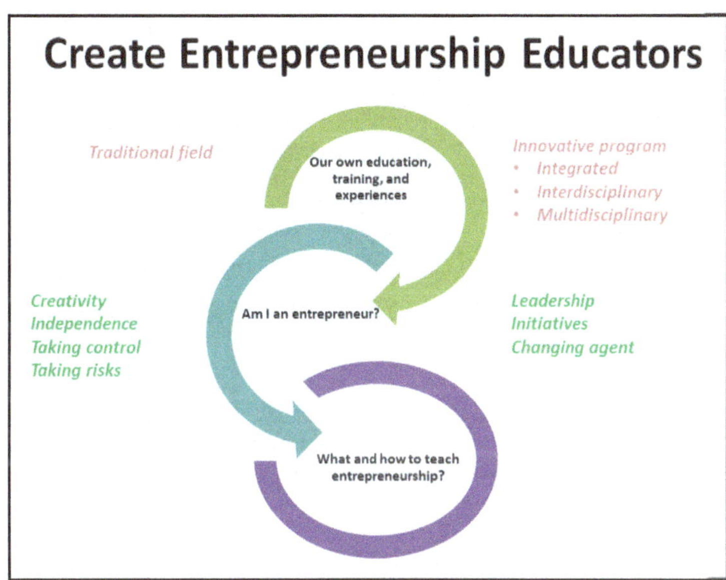

Courtesy of Chyi-lyi (Kathleen) Liang

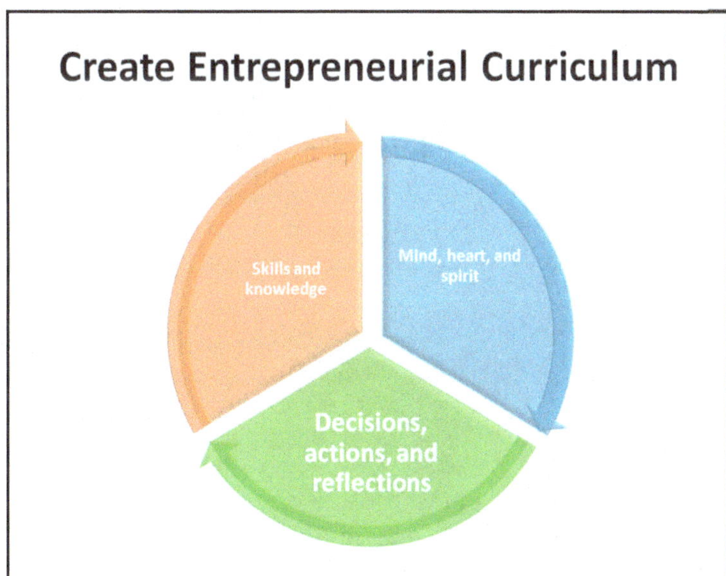

Courtesy of Chyi-lyi (Kathleen) Liang

An innovative entrepreneurship curriculum need to include three aspects:

- Teaching and learning about entrepreneurial skills and knowledge – how to work with people in a diverse environment; how to use existing and limited resources to create new value added products; and how to transform limited and restricted aspects into boundless opportunities.
- Nurturing and supporting entrepreneurial mindset and characteristics – from individuals' mind to heart to spirit.
- Informing and sharing decisions, actions, and reflections – from strategies to consequences.

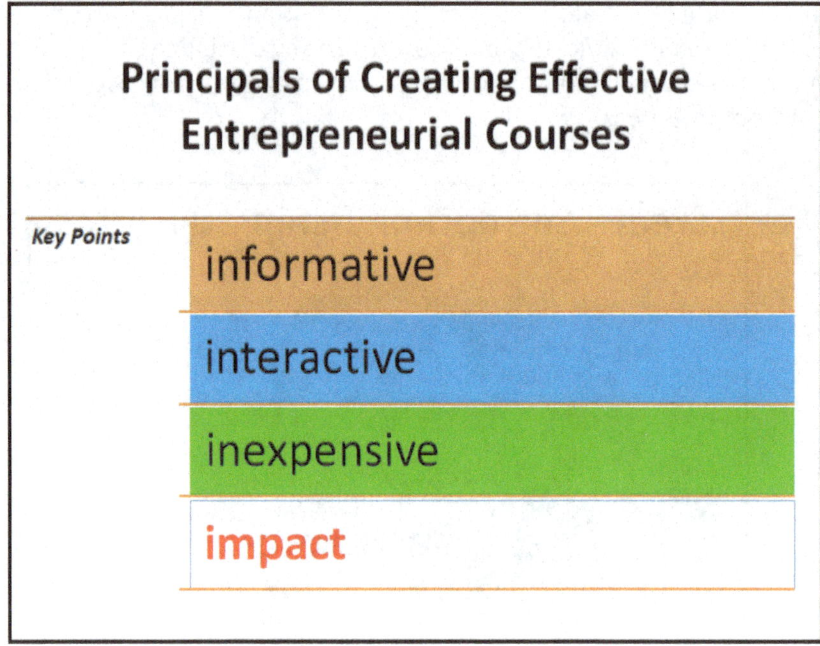

Courtesy of Chyi-lyi (Kathleen) Liang

The most effective way to create an entrepreneurial course is to make sure that:

- It contains sufficient and clear information to describe entrepreneurial individuals as well as entrepreneurial ventures; procedures to become an entrepreneurial thinker as well as an engaging member; and step-by-step guide to lead learners into the entrepreneurship domain.
- It has to be fun and interactive to offer learners direct contacts with team members, customers, community organizations, institutional offices, and other partners.
- It has to be inexpensive for institution administrators to buy in to the course activities.
- It has to use the minimum resources to generate the maximum impacts for institutions, communities, and learners.

For Other Organizations

Any organization can use this book as a guide book to create, design, and implement your own entrepreneurship curriculum or program. The contents in this book are flexible and informative. There are many youth development programs in the world, and many follow a similar path to assist young people to learn about creating their own ventures and opportunities. This book offers specific instructions to organize and operate small businesses in a college environment. However, organization leaders can modify procedures and instructions based on your own community needs, local policies, and background of the learners.

(To be collected by instructor on the first day of each semester after going through details in syllabus)

I have carefully and thoroughly reviewed the syllabus and all attached materials. I agree to follow the policies, to participate in all required course activities, and to contribute my effort with my best capacity.

Print Your Name ____

Sign Your Name ____

Date ____

Reflection Questions

What do you expect to learn from this course (learning goals)?

How do you plan to achieve your learning goals in this course?

Please list any questions to Dr. Liang.

The **teaching pedagogy** of Dollar Enterprise follows a unique learning model by integrating the Community Entrepreneurship theory (Team, Resource, Opportunity) with Experiential Learning (learning by engaging in action and decision making) and Service Learning (create positive impacts through services). Most of the learners begin with lecture-type courses, where students listen to lectures and take notes. Once the students are more familiar with concepts and definitions, they are ready to read cases and examples that cover other people's stories. This is the time period when students absorb information, digest information, and identify opportunities that might be triggered from existing stories and information.

Teachers often introduce discussions, debates, and other formats of interactions in classroom to motivate students to share their own ideas, perspectives, and inputs after reading and listening. Through a series of discussion and questions, students are expected to use existing materials and information to formulate their own concepts or frameworks corresponding to different subjects in their own thinking process. For example, once we read a story about how other people start their own art studio or landscape enterprise, students should be able to understand (1) what it takes to start an art studio or landscape enterprise, (2) how these people start their own businesses, (3) challenges and risks for these people to start their own business, and (4) returns and impacts of these businesses such as offering more local people job opportunities, offering training workshops for youth groups, and contributing to school programs to support education in art or landscape/environmental services.

The highest level of learning occurs when students are able to utilize reading materials or discussion topics to generate their own ideas to design, create, and implement new strategies to take actions in entrepreneurial opportunities. At this stage, students should be motivated and guided through the process to identify needs in their communities, identify resources and opportunities to support community economic/social mobility, and be able to directly link to community organizations and contribute to creating wealth.

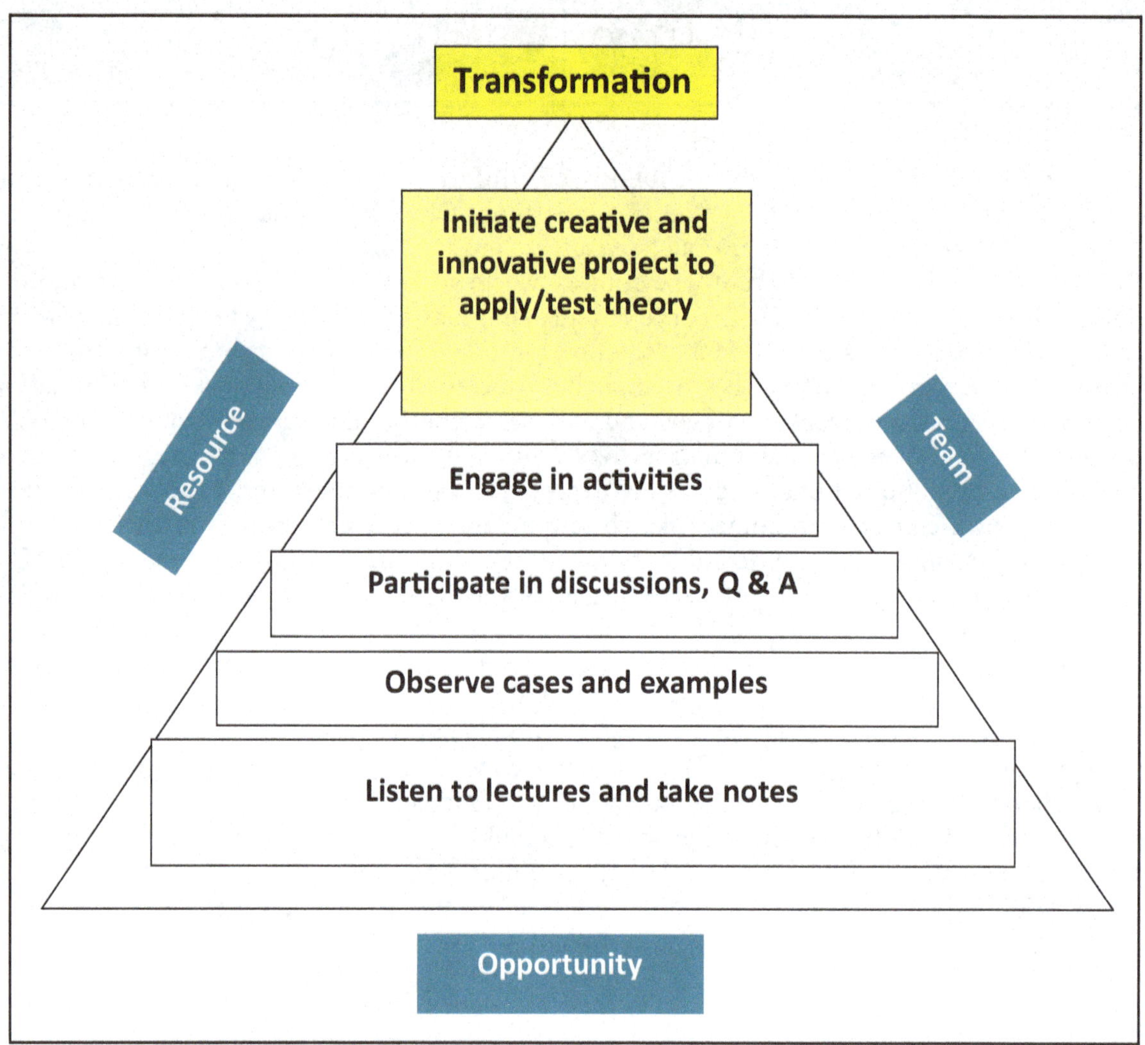

Courtesy of Chyi-lyi (Kathleen) Liang

Dollar Enterprise Learning Model

The key point is to create a dynamic learning environment in which theory and application are covered simultaneously.

Each student has the opportunity to go through this learning model with their own learning pace and style. We always start with the fundamental lectures, then students will engage in discussion and debate in the classroom, and finally students initiate and implement creative projects on campus to further apply/verify the theories.

Furthermore, using peer-to-peer assistance and evaluation, each student receives information and knowledge beyond textbook and class lecture. Without using multiple choice questions or true/false statements, every student responds to a series of essay-type questions every week regarding how different theory works (or does not work) given a set of assumptions and real-life based examples.

Education becomes a full circle when each individual thinks and responds to multiple aspects before reaching conclusions (Outside the Box), and has been challenged to reach her/his full capacity in critical thinking and decision-making.

The objectives of the Dollar Enterprise are to learn:

- The process to become a successful entrepreneur.
- What it takes to become a successful entrepreneur through a guided process of experiencing teamwork, business planning, challenges, failure, and rewards of being an entrepreneur.
- How to respond to risks, uncertainty, customers, collaborators, and regulatory issues.

Here are key elements to consider while developing Dollar Enterprise operations:

- **Development of the Theme for Dollar Enterprise.**

  The theme of Dollar Enterprise is to promote recycle, reuse, renew, and up-cycle. Students are encouraged to utilize *unwanted wastes*, modify the concepts of this *trash*, and create new value-added *treasure* for others.

- **Development of the Teamwork.**

  One of the most important things for any organization to be successful is to build a strong team. Each individual is expected to learn:

Leadership

    Listen to others

    Be patient and think before we talk

    Ask questions and provide feedback

    Keep a *to do* list with a reasonable timeline

    Set priorities and be flexible

    Joint decisions—share ideas, reach consensus, and negotiate

    Encourage open communication and adapt effective communication methods

Organizational structure

    Straight line style

    Triangle style

    Circle style

    Multi-layers style

Communication and Collaboration

    Share information in an open and respectful manner

    Convey message and make key points

    Use direct and clear contents

    Use graphs, tables, pictures, images, etc.

Achievable Goals (S.M.A.R.T. Goals)

    Be specific, measurable, attainable, reasonable, and timely

Love

- **Creative thinking.**

People often say: "Think outside the box." The real question should be: "Where is the box?" Creativity comes in all forms and concepts, and it exists in everyone's mind. The real issue is to assist individuals to explore and discover creative ideas, by looking at historical trend and by examining challenging issues in our daily life.

- **Analytical skills.**

A thinking process can be complicated. Learners tend to take information in, but not to process it further for deeper analysis. When students are planning and implementing Dollar Enterprise, we use the following steps to help students to analyze things systematically:

    (1) Understand how to create a feasible idea.

    (2) Understand how to transform an idea into a realistic concept.

    (3) Learn business skills, communication skills, and professionalism in workplace.

    (4) Play with numbers—records and impact.

- **Entrepreneurial activities.**

People often wonder: "What does it mean to be entrepreneurial?" Anyone can be entrepreneurial, and it is only a matter if we realize it or not. Being entrepreneurial usually means different things to different people. In most of the cases, it implies to step out of our comfort zone, and to try something that we have not tried before. In Dollar Enterprise, we encourage each individual to develop observation skills and research capacity to study what has been offered on campus. Based on their study, students need to generate concepts and to prove the concepts will work.

- **Networking skills.**

Everyone needs to work with a team in real life. The networking system in Dollar Enterprise includes campus administration, community organizations, and family and friends. Thanks to the development of social media, Dollar Enterprise is able to reach out to many individuals and organizations effectively. Students need to learn how to contact people using professional communication (e-mail, business letter, interview, and thank-you letter). Students also need to know how to work with individuals and organizations by creating a win-win strategy.

- **Contributions to society.**

The most important difference between general entrepreneurship and community entrepreneurship is in *building community asset*. Dollar Enterprise is committed to providing community partners as a resource to improve their services for others.

- **Have fun in learning!**

This is an introductory course, and we want each student to take advantage to enjoy the process while learning.

NOTES

NOTES

Every student in this class must return a copy of the following information **in the first week** of each semester:

1. Whether or not you have a driver's license—yes (which state) or no.
2. The name of your current health insurance company. If you are not the primary insured, please include the name of the primary insured (it is likely to be parents).
3. The name of your current automobile insurance company. If you are not the primary insured, please include the name of the primary insured.
4. Identify if you have your own vehicle on campus.

The instructor will assist you in applying for permits from Campus Enterprise (http://www.ncat.edu/divisions/business-and-finance/ce/) and other institutional organizations. The permits for locations should be applied for one semester ahead. The food permits will be applied for as soon as teams identify the food items and ingredients. It usually takes at least 2–3 weeks to apply for food permits. If products involve creating images, graphic design, wordings, or any other designs and communication, the instructor must review all designs before students could print on any products. The following offices on campus need to be informed prior to Dollar Enterprise activities:

1. Campus Enterprise.
2. Student Government Association (for special permission or reservation such as painting or chalking on the sidewalk).
3. Other clubs and student organizations (for space, events, and collaboration).
4. Dormitory Management Officers (if you will sell in the dorms).
5. All printed messages, wordings, and images must be pre-approved by the instructor before released to public.

All activities must follow the latest Code of Conduct of North Carolina Agricultural and Technical State University students and employees. Here is the link to the full document:

http://www.ncat.edu/legal/policies/sec3-human-resources/Sexual_Misconduct_Discrimination_Harassment_Sexual_Assault.pdf

The following information must be included in all documents and materials you present in public or to the instructor:

ABM 250   **Dollar Enterprise**

Developing and Operating a Business on Campus

Advisor: Dr. Chyi-lyi (Kathleen) Liang
Coltrane Hall 105 B   336 285 4683   cliang@ncat.edu

NOTES

NOTES

NOTES

NOTES

NOTES

The instructor will give each student in this class $1 as an initial investment.

No personal monetary donations are allowed.

Each student can contribute his/her own stuff, such as paper, tape, markers, cookware, small appliance, etc.

Students are also allowed to request for supplies and materials to be donated by local organizations. Most often students may work with their charity and corporate sponsors to gather donations.

Students need to earn enough income to purchase additional ingredients, supplies, and materials that will be directly invested in creating your products. You may not use earnings to purchase promotional materials (such as T-shirts, candy, or games) that are not direct ingredients for your products. Students who have contributed own investment must be paid back as soon as possible (usually the next day after purchase with receipts attached). ***No receipts, no reimbursement!***

By the end of the Dollar Enterprise activities in each semester, the instructor expects each student to return $2 that will be invested in the next class project and the Entrepreneurship Education Fund at the North Carolina A&T State University.

The starting time of Dollar Enterprise will be determined by instructor. Each semester we start Dollar Enterprise in different dates due to:

1. Seasonal weather—we often start Dollar Enterprise in late September in Fall semester when weather is appropriate and when we can take advantage of the Homecoming events. In the Spring semester, we need to wait until outdoor temperature is warm enough.

2. Once starting, each team must continue the work Monday through Friday, 5 days a week, between 8 a.m. and 5 p.m. according to your team schedule. **Each team must operate at least 3 hours daily not including the set up and closing**, and it does not need to be consecutive hours. Each team member needs to share balanced workload during the Dollar Enterprise process. For example, some people can sell at the table longer hours, some people can help make products more often, some people can write the business plan better, etc. Each team will make independent, collaborative decisions on each individual's role and responsibilities based on each person's strength and constraints. This must be clearly documented in team policy. Submit the team policy to instructor for approval prior to starting Dollar Enterprise.

For risks and liability issues, please consider university policy or institutional policy. Some examples include:

* The food stand and bake sale should stay away from food items such as dairy and meat products that have a spoilage factor. Always wear gloves and use clean water to wash your hands prior to and after serving customers. The person handling money should never touch food. No meat products are allowed. The campus dining service directors have worked hard to shape policy around potentially hazardous foods such as hot dogs. While hot dogs are some of the safest potentially hazardous foods, they still fall into that category based on risk assessment. Students are also not allowed to give away or sample potentially hazardous foods such as proteins due to the risk, liability, and lack of food safety documentation.

* Make sure to post the ingredients of food items in case some customers have an allergy or sensitivity. All perishable items such as dairy, fresh fruits, and vegetables, must be refrigerated on site. Do not sell overnight food items, drinks, or other perishable items.

* Assure that no personal services allowed, and respect personal space.

* Items to be sold or served will not include alcohol, cigarettes, drugs or any illegal item. No alcohol or drug references. No sexual expressive or conduct sexually suggestive. No gender/race/ethnic/sexual identity language that could be considered offensive. No use of any registered trademark, trade name, business identity, etc.

Entrepreneurship in general represents taking initiatives to generate new and unique concepts of products and/or services. People can be entrepreneurial given different environment in different situations. For example, entrepreneurial people often seek new jobs, new opportunities, new projects, or new challenges in life when they are not satisfied with existing positions. Being an entrepreneur does not necessarily mean to own a business. Being a business owner does not imply that you are an entrepreneur. Scholars have argued for many years about finding an appropriate definition for *entrepreneur* or *entrepreneurship*. Unfortunately, entrepreneurship is not a singular dimension of knowledge. It is a combination of knowledge and skills in multiple disciplines such as business, economics, psychology, technology, communication, and other scientific fields depending on the path of entrepreneurial interests and development. An entrepreneur often has a keen sense to explore opportunities, where innovation and creativity are transformed into real marketable products and/or services. However, many innovative ideas have vanished before they could be transformed into real commodities and/or services. The failure of an entrepreneurial path often links to lack of information, limited research and understanding of the market, and lack of resources and support. Entrepreneurship takes much more than an imagination, and it needs to be a balanced decision between taking chances and intelligent execution.

Entrepreneurship can be an exciting and mysterious subject to many people who have had dream ideas since childhood. Some of the dream ideas have the potential to be developed into unique and successful product and/or service concepts. These concepts can be further developed into successful enterprises whether it is a commercial enterprise or a non-profit organization. It is essential for a successful entrepreneur to be well prepared for success and failure. Unfortunately sometimes a dream idea can also become a nightmare for people who do not have adequate skills and knowledge to capitalize on opportunities.

Being a successful entrepreneur involves tremendous effort, commitment, and dedication. Those who have dreamed about being their own boss one day, always wonder what it would be like to actually start and run their own business. Common questions for entrepreneur-want-to-be to ask most likely include:

- Do I have what it takes to become successful with respect to my personality and characteristics?
- Will my idea really work? How do I know?
- If I am not happy with my current job, would it be better if I have my own business?
- Do I have the knowledge, skills, and experiences to own a business?
- Do I have enough resources and support to be a successful business owner?
- What do I need to do to start my own business? And where should I start?
- What if something goes wrong after I start the business, and what do I need to do to prevent/minimize the loss?

Dollar Enterprise, an integrated and unique activity offered by the Department of Community Development and Applied Economics through a course "Introduction to Community Entrepreneurship" provides a perfect opportunity for young entrepreneurs to gain firsthand experiences about new venture creation and *community* development. Educators have raised several issues relating to entrepreneurship education in the United States, for example:

- The focus of entrepreneurship education has evolved significantly from business-focused discipline to multi-disciplinary and inter-disciplinary education. However, significant gaps exist between curriculum design and deliverables. It is challenging for educators to create a set of curriculum to cover knowledge and skills for entrepreneurship—more important, it is difficult to define what we should teach and how we should teach entrepreneurship.

- Many educators are not as prepared to transfer knowledge and skills across disciplines. Most of the professors and instructors are trained in our own discipline. Educators do not have sufficient opportunities to encounter or practice multi-disciplinary or inter-disciplinary teaching environment prior to our employment. Even many educators could be entrepreneurial, we might not have been exposed to a real entrepreneurial environment in which we could share knowledge and experiences across disciplines.
- There is lack of incentive and motivation to promote entrepreneurship education. Since entrepreneurship consists of collaboration across multiple disciplines, it is often confusing to traditional academic field with respect to rewarding and encouraging educators who work across disciplines.
- Most of the entrepreneurship education focuses more on business knowledge, and not enough on developing a process of entrepreneurial learning. Teaching entrepreneurship is not to teach everyone to be entrepreneurs. Entrepreneurship education is about informing learners of the process of being entrepreneurial, the opportunities of being entrepreneurial, the resources needed to be entrepreneurial, and the consequences of being entrepreneurial. Unfortunately most of the entrepreneurship textbooks remain focused on conventional information about management, business planning, venture creation, marketing, and financial analysis.

There is an emerging need for innovative pedagogy to teach entrepreneurship across disciplines. According to industry reports and labor market demand, the future generation of entrepreneurs must understand the triggers influencing the development of organizational structures and be able to respond to the need of future commodity/labor markets. Educators need to be entrepreneurial first while designing and implementing curriculum that will:

- Build stronger and more competitive labor force.
- Develop more creative and resourceful employees and employers.
- Break down the barriers in learning and sharing knowledge across disciplines.
- Help learners learn *how to learn*, instead of *contents*.

Some limitations of the entrepreneurship education in the United States involve, for example:

- Business Schools dominate in entrepreneurship programs.
- Community colleges and technical centers are catching up with more creative approaches to deliver the entrepreneurship information.
- Limited entrepreneurship curriculum is available in non-business disciplines.
- Limited programs are available in K–12.

NOTES

NOTES

THEORY OF COMMUNITY ENTREPRENEURSHIP

In general, Entrepreneurship represents the process of transforming limited resources to value-added goods and services by seeking and/or creating new opportunities in the market or/and in an institution. Entrepreneurship exists everywhere and can happen at any time. Creating a business is only one dimension of interpreting Entrepreneurship. People can be entrepreneurial with or without creating/owning businesses. Entrepreneurial individuals often are willing to explore the potential of generating goods, services, and knowledge for others. These individuals are also willing to take actions considering opportunities and resource constraints. Here are a few things that we can compare and contrast when teaching and learning about Community Entrepreneurship:

- What is general Entrepreneurship?

Entrepreneurship is a process of transformation for individuals and enterprises. This process involves thinking, developing, acting, decision-making, and strategizing. Anyone can become an entrepreneur, and anyone can formulate dream ideas over time. How did entrepreneurs discover the dream idea? The most common way is to learn from the past. People identify patterns or unusual events when looking back in time:

- Something had a repetitive trend in the history (such as fashion),
- Something happened unexpectedly and created a lot of curiosity (such as virus and infectious diseases),
- Something we used all the time but did not work very well (such as typewriter), and
- Something could make our lives easier but did not exist in real life (such as potential sources of alternative energy).

It takes someone who is passionate and committed to the dream idea to further derive a concept for the dream. The concept of an idea usually describes specific features, characteristics, and functions. For an idea of a product, the concept includes size, color, material, usefulness, design, and other specific information related to this product. For an idea of a service, the concept should explain the nature of the service, what it takes to deliver the service, who will perform the service, potential benefits related to the service, and other specific functions of the service.

Once the concept is drafted and finalized, the next step is to create a sample or a prototype using the concept. This stage often involves interactions with potential customers or users who could provide feedback to entrepreneurs regarding the proposed goods and services. Entrepreneurs also need to conduct intensive market and industry research to gather more information about competition, target customers' profile, customers' preference and purchasing patterns, potential size of the market, industry trend, and other information that will support the development of proposed goods and services.

When entrepreneurs can prove the opportunity and market potential of proposed goods and services, the final step is to create a *circle of entrepreneurial decisions*. Entrepreneurs need to decide how much resource it would take to produce the goods and services, including monetary investment and infrastructure. Organizing and managing an entrepreneurial team is critical for success. Sharing intelligence, responsibilities, and skills will provide a more effective, efficient, and sustainable working relationship between entrepreneurs and the team. After the goods and services are introduced to the market, entrepreneurs need to evaluate the outcomes based on sales, values, performance, satisfaction, or other indicators. Entrepreneurs learn from the experience, whether it is a success or failure, and begin the modification of the idea and concept by re-assessing market opportunities.

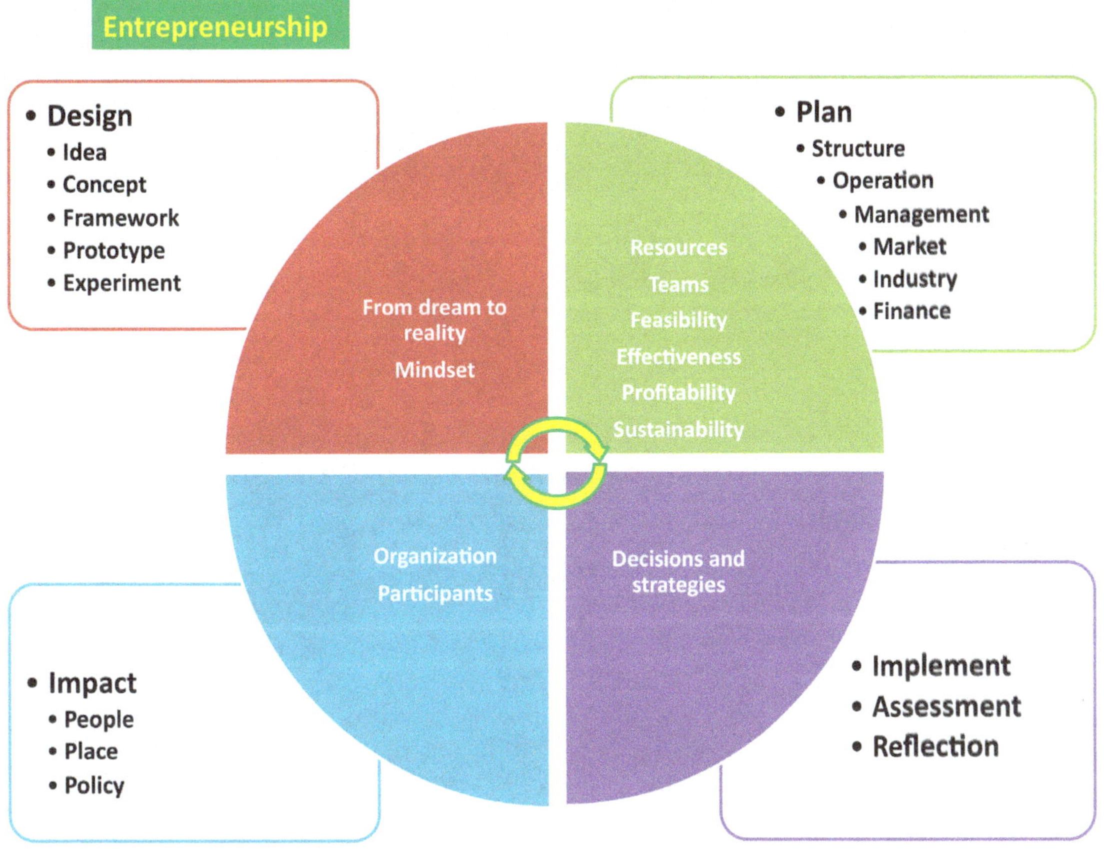

Courtesy of Chyi-lyi (Kathleen) Liang

- What is Community Entrepreneurship?

Community Entrepreneurship involves a similar process as general Entrepreneurship. The major difference between Community Entrepreneurship and general Entrepreneurship lies in the sense of *community involvement and transformation of the community*. Community Entrepreneurship focuses on community building and capacity improvement, by strengthening the root of entrepreneurship in each community. Each community has its own characteristics and culture. Some communities are in rural areas where small family businesses are the norm of the culture, and most of the residents have known each other for generations. Other communities are located in large metropolitan areas where advanced technology companies and higher income residents dominate. Entrepreneurs interact with different communities in many ways—creating new jobs, supporting existing jobs, improving income and employment situations, stimulating organizational collaborations, and encouraging innovation and creativity in general. Community Entrepreneurship represents the links between entrepreneurs, organizations, and people given the constraints of resources and opportunities.

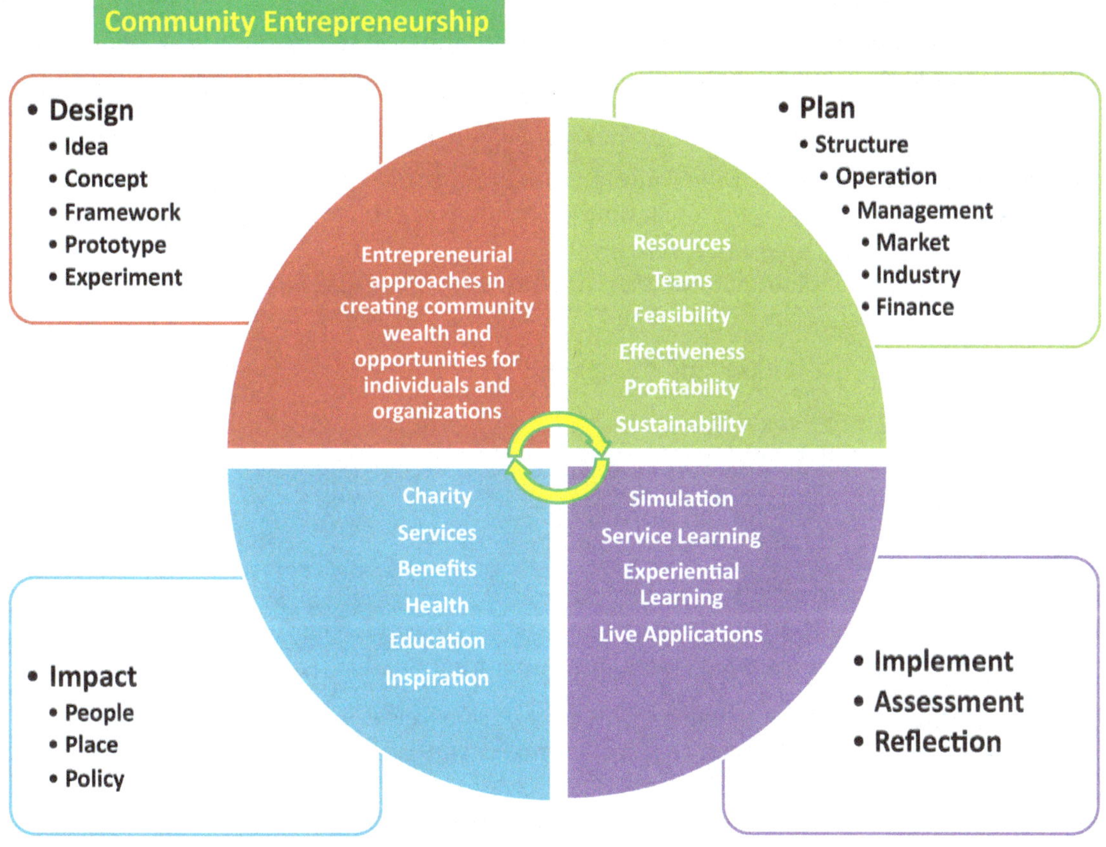

Courtesy of Chyi-lyi (Kathleen) Liang

- Why and how do people become entrepreneurs?

This is a million-dollar question that researchers have been arguing for a long time. There has been no agreement among researchers with respect to specific reasons for people to become entrepreneurs. Are entrepreneurs born with the talents? Is there a general profile for entrepreneurs? Are certain people more likely to become entrepreneurs than others? Many myths associated with entrepreneurs and their decisions are yet to be explored. One thing we know for sure is that entrepreneurs do create dynamic transformations for our society.

Based on existing literature, we believe that entrepreneurs are those who love their own ideas and want to make something happen. They are passionate, dedicated, and committed to their own ideas and actions. They have the tenacity, perseverance, confidence, and motivation to pursue new ideas and opportunities. They tend to be realistic and optimistic when evaluating the market potential for their creation, whether it is a product or a service. However literature has also discussed many reasons for entrepreneurs to fail while seeking opportunities—being too ambitious, too optimistic, and too dominating in the decision-making process.

Generally speaking, people become entrepreneurs given an integrated set of factors—employment and economic environment, personal traits, and family situation. Many workers have been laid off from the job market due to a declining demand in certain positions. Many employees have been displaced in the job market (which means their skills and knowledge might not be the best fit for their current positions), because they could not afford not to have a job. When the overall economy faces downward trends, people are forced to be creative in finding other opportunities. Someone with the entrepreneurial characteristics and personal traits, and sometimes pressure from the family, could easily break through the economic barriers and become entrepreneurial.

Anyone can be an entrepreneur, but not everyone can be successful. Learning about how to be a successful entrepreneur takes time and effort. The key to success involves:

- 3 D's: determination, dedication, and discipline.
- Practice makes perfection.
- Behave and visualize what you want to achieve every moment.
- Live in the dream and act on it all the time.
- Be open to criticism and appreciate comments.
- Always think from other people's perspectives.

- How do entrepreneurs generate value added for our community?

A value-added product or service usually includes *monetary rewards* and/or *satisfaction* for both producers and customers. Beyond financial rewards, entrepreneurs offer products and services to help other people and organizations to reach their goals. The overall satisfaction for entrepreneurs and their customers goes beyond the monetary exchange. It is the interactions about working together to improve the community social and economic situation.

LEARNING EXPECTATIONS AND SERVICE REQUIREMENTS

At the end of the semester, students will be expected to:

- Develop critical thinking and understand the relationship between entrepreneurship, our society, and personal goals.
- Gain knowledge about the variations in entrepreneurship theories and practices.
- Identify decision-making strategies relating to entrepreneurship and community development issues.
- Know how to formulate analytical and entrepreneurial problems in decision making and be able to apply such knowledge in real life.

NOTE:

- Once you finalize team members, no one will be allowed to switch teams.
- Dollar Enterprise is a real business operation on campus for one month. Once each team starts the Dollar Enterprise process, each team must operate at least 3 hours every day, Monday through Friday between 8 a.m. to 5 p.m. (not including 30 minutes pre-operation preparation and 30 minutes post-operation clean up), and the work schedule (team and individual) must be formulated and agreed by all team members.
- Once schedule is finalized, you may not change the operation hours. Once you start the business, you may not close the business for any reason except a real emergency defined by university or institutional risk management and policies. Any uncertain events must be cleared by Dr. Liang.
- Disciplines for team members must be clearly defined by your team policy and approved by instructor.
- Each Dollar Enterprise team will identify a local charity organization to work with. We will directly contribute to charity—donate all profits and provide services.
- Each team will identify a local charity, contact the charity with instructor's assistance, understand the needs of the charity, and design a unique service component through Dollar Enterprise. Each team member also has more opportunities to contribute time, skills, and knowledge by directly working with their community organizations.
- We are looking for small to medium non-profit organizations with a social mission. Examples are youth and family service organizations, senior centers, animal shelters, food shelves, and homeless shelters. We do not make donations to private use, personal use, or non-profit without proper registration records with the states.

Service items may include:

1. Assisting or participating in organizing events and workshops.
2. Offering volunteer services in youth, family, senior related activities.
3. Raising awareness of social issues by distributing brochures, pamphlets, and flyers.
4. Participating in food drive, clothes drive, diaper drive, and other collections.

Each individual in each team is required to keep a journal to document:

1. Each individual is required to contribute 10 hours of services in one semester. Service categories are defined broadly between instructor, team members, and charity organization.
2. Each individual must log all hours of services, service items, and ask charity organization manager to sign on the log every time to verify services.
3. Team members can provide services individually or with a sub group, whichever is the most convenient format for each team upon agreement with all members.

Sample letter to be prepared and agreed on between each team and charity organization (this letter must be collected by instructor within the first 3 weeks of each semester).

CREATE A DRAFT OF SERVICE LEARNING AGREEMENT

Brainstorm an Idea (1 day)

Brainstorm is often the first stage for entrepreneurial activities. We ask questions "how" and "why" when we observe interesting situations and events. It takes someone with a special mindset to push further to develop an idea.

It is often easier to identify *how* and *why,* and it will be more challenging for us to understand *so what*. Successful entrepreneurs ask a lot of questions in all situations, and they will not be discouraged easily just because people might respond to them *well, that is a stupid idea, this is impossible,* or *that is not doable.* Brainstorming should be open and nonjudgmental. Encourage as many ideas as possible before evaluating them!

In the past, we had many success stories and failure cases in our Dollar Enterprise activities. There is no formula to achieve success. We define success when:

1. Team members work very well together. Each individual is taking on a fair share of workload. All team members communicate effectively and efficiently. All members keep everyone informed all the time. When someone needs help, other members are willing to lend a hand.

2. Daily operation goes very smoothly according to planned schedule. Team members never skip a day, never change a shift, and never ignore team procedures.

3. Products are popular and strongly supported by a sustainable customer base. Products fulfill customers' need. Prices are reasonable and affordable. Weekly special promotions and new products attract customers' attention and interests. Team members are able to grow customer base on weekly basis.

4. Financial returns match with the growing sales and customers' interests. Team's production and sales strategies meet customers' demand.

There is no guaranteed success in Dollar Enterprise. The same business idea may work in one semester, but it may fail in another semester. A sample list of Dollar Enterprise operations includes:

- Grilled cheese sandwich, crepe, muffin, pie, cookies, Chinese dumplings and spring rolls, coffee, ice tea, lemonade, fresh apple cider, hot tea, root beer float, hot chocolate, vegetable soup and chili, trail mix, waffle, and homemade cake.

- Jewelry, handmade mugs and cups, tie dye products, up-cycled clothes and accessories, handmade cards and stationary, handmade paper flower, resale shop, arts, photos, buttons, coasters, table clothes and matching napkins, and sweaters and hats.

Write down a few ideas you would like to share.

Why do you think these ideas would work well?

What are some potential issues associated with each idea?

Once you have an idea, we need to think about what we have on campus and where our opportunities might be.

- **What kind of products we already have on campus sold by different venues?**
  - This relates to the analysis of our competitors on campus. We perform a SWOT analysis to gather information about our competitors' strength and weakness given their products. And we look at the opportunities for Dollar Enterprise teams to offer something different in quality and design.
- **What is the quality of these existing products on campus?**
  - We need to review the materials and ingredients of existing products on campus. Sometimes we might be able to build a collaborative effort with other vendors on campus. For example, campus dining service might be able to provide ice to Dollar Enterprise teams for no charge. In return, we acknowledge the support from campus dining service.
- **Can we offer something different from what we already have on campus?**
- **What will be the best way to develop and sustain our business?** Are we creating a product that will attract new customers every day, or are we creating a product that we will secure a loyal customer base?
- **Do we have the capacity and the skills to create better products for our students, faculty, staff, and visitors?**
  - Dollar Enterprise is a small operation compared with other businesses on campus. We need to make sure we have sufficient inventory and options for our customers to shop. With 8–10 people in each team, the team members' time management capacity will be the key to sustain production and operation.
- **Do we have a competitive advantage or comparative advantage to sell our products?**
  - Competitive advantage represents the niche we are offering through Dollar Enterprise production. Comparative advantage usually relates to lower costs of production compared with our competitors, or using alternative materials/ingredients to create better products.
- **Can we create collaborative competitive advantage between all Dollar Enterprise teams?**
  - It helps sometimes if Dollar Enterprise teams can work together to jointly promote the whole class. For example, the grilled cheese sandwich team may work with the coffee team to create a package deal. The root beer float team works with the handmade mug team to offer a joint product.

Now let us work on these activities!

NOTES

The purposes of brainstorming activities are:

- **To assist students in forming specific ventures for the class.**

   Ask each student to generate business ideas from individual perspectives. Think about the type of business that you would like to create in this class. Each student in this class should identify one or two business ideas that he or she believes would offer unique benefits to customers (primarily people on campus such as faculty, staff, and students).

- **To facilitate team formation and team building.**

   The instructor does not assign individuals to teams. Instead, students form teams based on similar interests and business ideas. The instructor collects individual ideas, separates them into categories, and students use these categories to form initial teams with approximately 8 to 10 individuals per team.

Here are a few things to prompt your thinking about the business idea:

- Our business activities are for course work only (nonprofit) and must follow the University Codes (safety, security, etc.).
- All business activities must be conducted on campus, and sales must be completed in four weeks (the specific time period of the operation will be announced in class).
- We will not provide any personal services or create any businesses that involve personal property.
- We will not create any products involving live animals.
- Arts and crafts must use recyclable and reusable materials.
- We do not order inventory from others. Students must create/make your own products using original design.
- Food production and sales must be pre-approved by Campus Food Service managed by Sodexho. It takes two to three weeks to file the paperwork.
- If your business idea needs to use any equipment or facilities on campus (such as tables, chairs, classrooms, etc.), there might be substantial costs involved. Try to avoid using these things on campus! Bring in your own tables and chairs if necessary.
  - No automobile should be involved without approval (whether you use it for transportation or services).
  - No alcohol, tobacco, or drug references. Do not sell anything, refer to, or link to these issues.
  - No sexually expressive/suggestive conduct.
  - No gender/race/ethnic/sexual identity language that could be considered offensive.
  - No use of any registered trademark, trade name, business identity, etc.

Be as simple as possible!

Your Name: _______________________________

Please Describe Your Business Idea Here

Describe clearly the products or services you propose for Dollar Enterprise. Include materials and ingredients that you will need to create this product.

Please list 5 reasons that you think your products or services will work on campus.

If you are flexible and open to other business ideas, please indicate so here:

Use Information Gathered From Brainstorm Session to Create Teams (1 day)

After we gather the ideas from each student, the instructor will work with Teaching Assistant to sort ideas by similarities into small groups.

The instructor posts the Dollar Enterprise venture categories in class, and Teaching Assistant organizes the initial team members (8–10 individuals in each group) based on similar interests or ideas.

Students will view the initial team assignment in class. If any team is under the minimum required members (8) or above the maximum required members (10), students will have an opportunity to restructure their teams through interpersonal negotiations. The negotiation methods include using personal constraints and professional requests.

Once the initial Dollar Enterprise teams are finalized, the instructor will facilitate the following types of activities.

- Getting to Know You—collect and exchange personal information.
- Ice Breaker Exercise.
  - Share personal interests and hobby, family background and history, cultural differences, and communities where they come from originally.
  - Identify personal traits and characteristics.
  - Share previous and/or current working experiences—part-time or full-time jobs that each person has worked.
  - Share personal skills, knowledge, and experience to identify each individual's strength and limitation. (It is very important to share openly what each person is willing to do, and what each person is definitely not willing to do.)
  - Share each person's communication strategies—it is critical to establish a commonly agreed method to communicate with each other. Some people use Facebook and texts, while others may not have a Facebook page. Each member needs to be very honest about what the best methods would be to connect with others.
  - Share each person's communication style—each member needs to describe communication style and preference, such as open discussion, private conversation, or tendency to procrastinate.

NOTES

NOTES

Do You Want to Switch Teams? (1 day)

STEP 3

After initial team members are assigned to each group, each person will have one day to consider if he/her would like to change teams. To switch to a different team, here are the rules:

1. You may not switch to a team with more than 10 members already.
2. You need the new team's permission to join them.
3. Check with new team that you want to join, and understand existing members' strength and limitation—are you going to be a good match and contributor to this new team?
4. The final members of each team may not have more than 2 athletes who need to travel frequently for games and competitions.
5. The final members of each team may not include more than 2 international students (from the same country or from different countries).
6. Avoid being in a team with your close friends, roommates, relatives, etc.—avoid conflict of interests and potential biases against others.

Team Name: _______________________________

Name of Members	Phone Number	E-Mail Address

Finalize Team Members, Members' Duties, and Team Working Structure (1 day)

Each team needs to assign specific Team Member's Duties and Responsibilities even though everyone works together. Each team needs to select a team leader, marketing leader, production leader, operation and management leader, finance leader, record keeper, and other positions.

- Team leader—coordinate step-by-step procedures of Dollar Enterprise.
- Marketing leader—coordinate advertising and promotion activities.
- Production leader—coordinate purchasing ingredients and materials, product design, inventory management, and scheduling daily/weekly production and members.
- Finance leader—gather data from daily costs, sales, donation, and calculate daily net earnings (profits). Daily profit is the difference between daily sales and daily costs, plus donations.
- Communication leader—take charge of daily communication and keep records of communication information, arrange team meetings, and follow up conflict and negotiation.

Use Individual's Talent, Interests, and Skills

Consider the information your team has gathered before, make a list to match assigned roles/responsibilities with personal talent, interests, and skills. Each team member can contribute to the team effort—let them, and encourage participation.

Consider Individual's Work Style and Communication Style

Some people have great personality to be leaders, while others may prefer to receive specific tasks and orders. Learning styles and communication styles are critical to a team's success. Let us use graphs, photos, and fun games to explore our learning styles and communication styles!

NOTES

NOTES

Collect Individual's Availability

To accommodate each person's tasks and skills, we need to consider each person's existing schedule for schoolwork and real world jobs. Making a list to show each person's availability will help each team decide who would be better to work in different roles.

Time management is critical for the success of Dollar Enterprise. Each member needs to be honest about time limitation before making a serious commitment with the team.

NOTES

Team Name: _______________________________

Name of Members	Job Title	Responsibilities

Identify a Team Structure

- There are different types of organizational structure for each team to adapt:
  - Type 1—straight line style

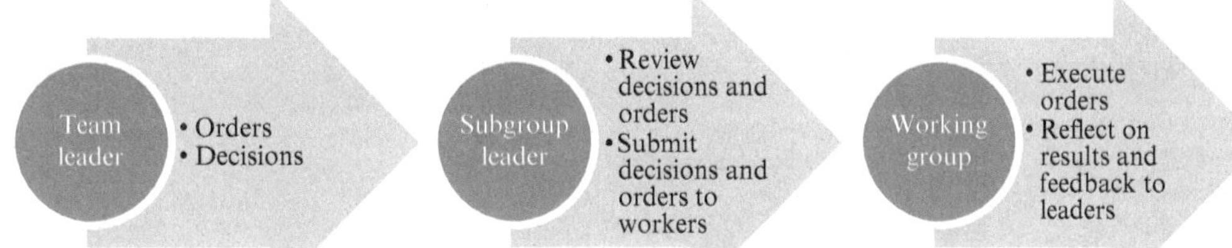

  - Type 2—triangle or hierarchy style

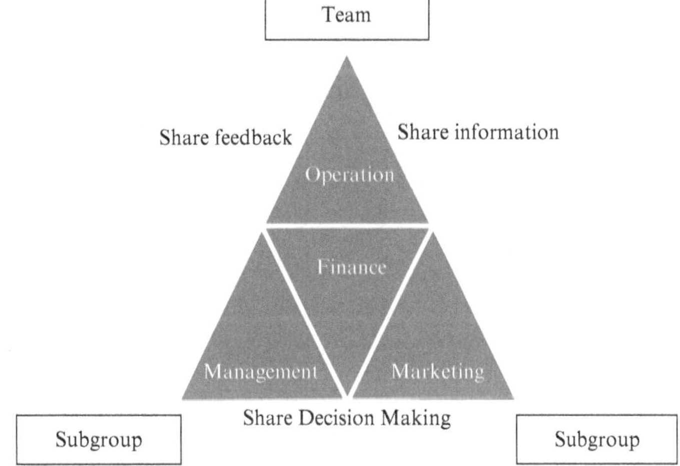

  - Type 3—circle style

Graphics Courtesy of Chyi-Iyi (Kathleen) Liang

Team Name: ________________________

Which team structure will you follow? Draw your own structure and identify each individual in your structure.

Information Returned to the Instructor

Initial Daily Work Hours by Individuals—Print Your Last Name Clearly by Time

	Monday	Tuesday	Wednesday	Thursday	Friday
8:00 a.m.					
8:15					
8:30					
8:45					
9:00					
9:15					
9:30					
9:45					
10:00					
10:15					
10:30					
10:45					
11:00					
11:15					
11:30					
11:45					

Initial Daily Work Hours by Individuals—Print Your Last Name Clearly by Time

	Monday	Tuesday	Wednesday	Thursday	Friday
12:00 p.m.					
12:15					
12:30					
12:45					
1:00					
1:15					
1:30					
1:45					
2:00					
2:15					
2:30					
2:45					
3:00					
3:15					
3:30					
3:45					
4:00					
4:15					
4:30					
4:45					
5:00 p.m. (close)					

Create Team Policy (1 day)

Define a Team Policy

A good and clear team policy will assist each member to complete tasks on time and to improve team efficiency in communication, production, operation, and management. It is important for each team to design and vote on your own policy to hold each member accountable.

Each team may dismiss any member who does not follow your own team policy after providing sufficient evidence and presenting to the instructor. Dismissed members will leave team immediately, may not join other teams, and will receive no grades from the course.

General Contents in a Team Policy

- Balance teamwork and individual's responsibility—list things clearly for each person to do.
- Define quality of work and products clearly.
- Describe communication frequency, responding rules, and professional language.
- Describe rewards for extra effort and contribution.
- Describe consequences, warning, and discipline for lack of effort and lack of professionalism.

NOTES

NOTES

Create your own team policy:

Cover Page

Name of the Team

____

Date

____

Print names of all members: Signatures of all team members:

_____________________________   _____________________________

_____________________________   _____________________________

_____________________________   _____________________________

_____________________________   _____________________________

_____________________________   _____________________________

_____________________________   _____________________________

_____________________________   _____________________________

_____________________________   _____________________________

_____________________________   _____________________________

Attach a copy of team policy to the cover page and return to instructor

Identify a Charity Organization for Service Learning Hours and Donation (1 day)

Each team needs to finalize charity you want to work with, and return a letter of agreement as described on the following page.

Design and Create Products Relating to Pricing Strategies (3 days)

In this stage, each team is required to finalize products or services that will be provided. The instructor will facilitate the following activities:

- What Are We Selling? What is our value proposition?
- Who Would Buy and Who Would Use?
- What Materials Would We Need and Where Could We Find These Materials?
- Why Are We Selling This Stuff?

To determine appropriate prices to charge, entrepreneurs often consider 4 factors:

1. How much can my customers afford to pay for our products?
2. How much will it cost us to make each product? (Rule = unit cost must be no more than 30% of your price. If you charge $1 for a cookie, you should spend less than 30 cents to make that cookie.)
3. How much will my customers be willing to pay for our products?
4. What are my competitors charging for the same or similar products?

It is extremely important to set the prices appropriately to at least cover production costs and other operating expenses. Often we control the cost per product to be no more than 30% of the price we charge.

We offer potential customers an opportunity to test students' products. The instructor often arranges sample testing in class time period, and ask the whole class to give each team feedback. We can also arrange a special campus event to test our products (for example, Love an Entrepreneur Day). The most important thing is to contact our customers to preview the products and give teams constructive feedback. Be observant and willing to change your product.

There are many free or less expensive sources for you to gather materials and ingredients. Be imaginative but do not steal!

The instructor organizes shopping trips for each team, and introduces teams to local stores that offer discounted items. Here is a list of stores and organizations that you may visit:

- Goodwill stores.
- Salvation Army retail shops.
- Recycle stores.
- Consignment store.
- Secondhand stores.
- Dollar stores.
- Local solid waste disposal outlets.
- Your own closets and rooms.
- Friends, family, and relatives.
- Material salvage outlets/centers.
- Local businesses.
- Nonprofit organizations.

The questions listed above are common questions entrepreneurs need to respond to while preparing for a new venture. The new venture creation process begins with the understanding of the business life cycle (also known as the product life cycle). A business cycle represents the development of the products and the business. There are several stages in the business cycle that each Dollar Enterprise team will experience:

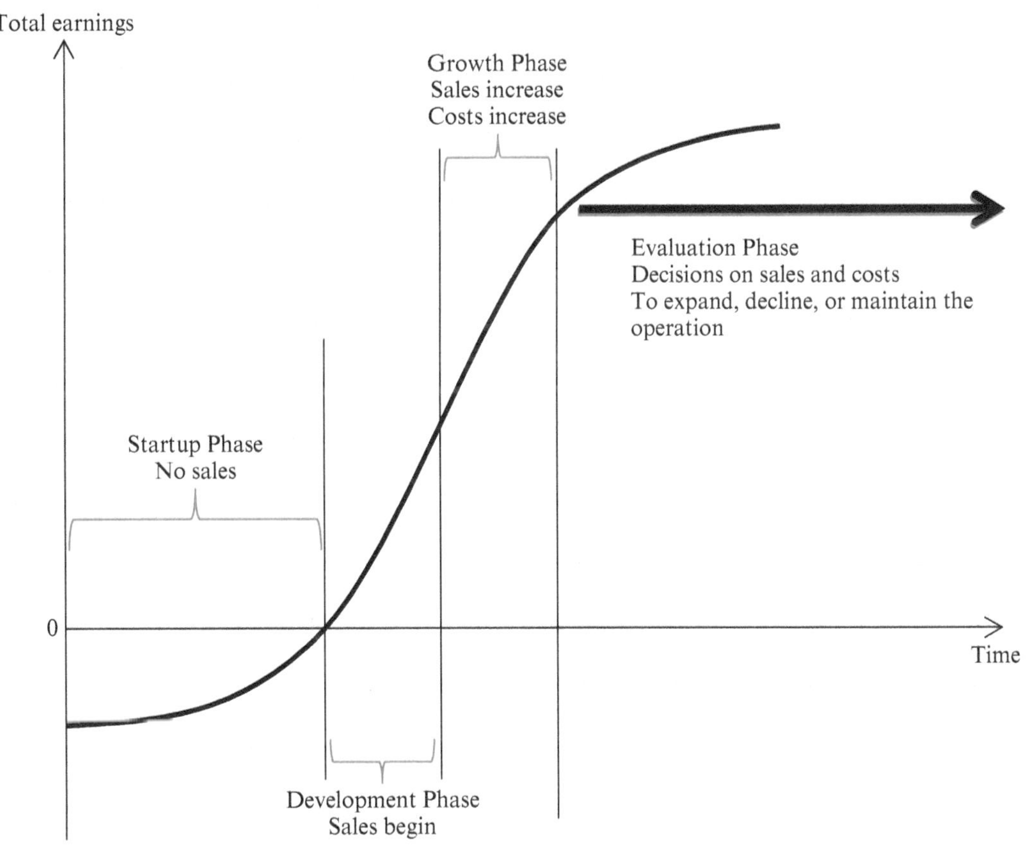

Courtesy of Chyi-lyi (Kathleen) Liang

Interestingly, the business cycle also mirrors the emotional changes for entrepreneurs in the process of new venture creation:

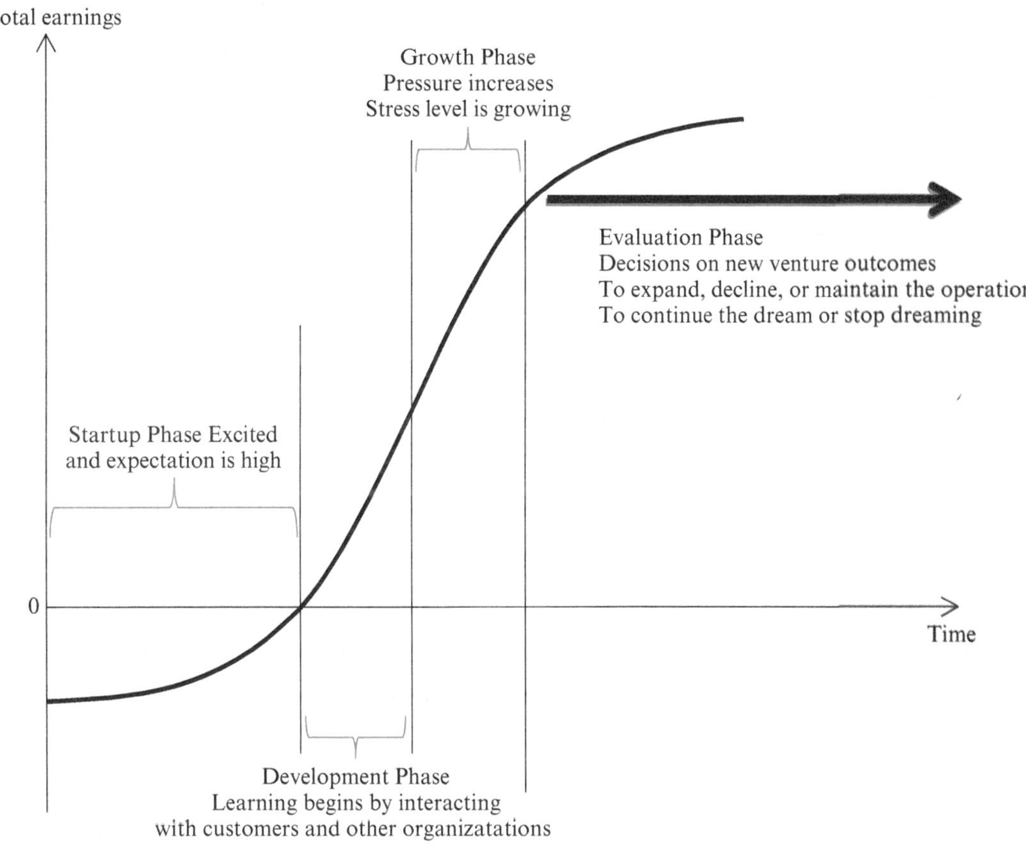

Courtesy of Chyi-lyi (Kathleen) Liang

- What are we selling?

- Who would buy and who would use?

- What materials would we need and where could we find these materials?

- Why are we selling this stuff?

Sample Menu for Food Products

Each food team needs to create your own menu to describe your food products, ingredients, allergy warnings, and sources of ingredients.

Sample Ingredient list (All food items must include allergy warning labels)

Necessary Materials/Ingredients
Honey, maple syrup, peanut butter, chocolate chips (semi-sweet melted morsels), cinnamon, coconut shavings, tea leaves, oats, dried fruit, nuts (almonds, cashews, peanuts), hot water, cups, and plastic bags

Necessary Materials/Ingredients
Peanut butter, Chocolate Rice Krispies, Rice Krispies, chocolate chips, Fruit Loops, Cinnamon Toast Crunch, marshmallow, powder sugar, Chex Cereal, Oreos, white chocolate, oats, honey, butter, brown sugar, salt, vanilla, dried cranberry, dried apples

Necessary Materials/Ingredients
Zucchini, apples, pumpkin puree, cinnamon, eggs, oil (vegetable), baking powder, baking soda, vanilla extract, water, brown sugar, butter, allspice, sugar (white), flour, salt, ground nutmeg, ground cloves, walnuts, tomatoes, onion, cilantro, garlic, ginger, lime juice, jalapeño pepper, vinegar, cucumber, green bell peppers, pickling salt, dill weed, red chili peppers, alum, green beans, pecan, blueberries, and other fresh fruits and vegetables

Sample Materials for Arts and Crafts

Necessary Materials/ Ingredients	—Candy (Halloween promotion) —Coaster (wooden and tile with pictures on top of round or square ~4" x 4") —Origami garland (5 cranes or 3' string)

Necessary Materials/Ingredients	Donated pens, spokes, bike tires, wine corks, bracelets, photo holder, page holder, pin pen, flowers, and money tree

Necessary Materials/Ingredients	—Mason Jars (various sizes) —Old records (various ages; old, new, condition, colors—will take whatever we can get) —Paper maché (glue, water, newspaper) —Old sheet music —Art supplies (glitter, old ribbon, paint brushes) —Candy from Costco (bags in bulk) *Cookies Week: (for Halloween?)

This letter is an example if teams would like to request donations from community partners. Here is a sample letter asking for donations (gift cards, in kind, or others):

Date

Key contact person and Organization name

Address

Dear Director:

I am a Professor at the North Carolina A&T State University teaching the Dollar Enterprise course. I am the founder of Dollar Enterprise, and this program has been recognized as one of the best entrepreneurship courses in America. I have designed an innovative learning strategy to assist students in planning, starting, and running a new venture on campus. The purpose of Dollar Enterprise is to provide students an opportunity utilizing $1 per person to experience what it is like to be entrepreneurial—to have their own new ventures and to deal with the challenges and risks that every entrepreneur faces—by working in teams with limited resources. All proceeds generated by Dollar Enterprise activities are donated to local charities.

My student team is seeking donations from your organization and your support. Here is the information about the team, the contact person, and the donation items we need:

Name of the team:

Contact person (name, address, and phone number):

Items needed (provide a detailed list of everything you are asking for):

The following is our institutional tax number for writing off your donation on your taxes:

NCAT Federal ID number will be provided to students in class

Again, my students and I appreciate your consideration and support!

Sincerely,

Kathleen Liang
Kellogg Distinguished Professor of Sustainable Agriculture
Director, Center for Environmental Farming Systems
North Carolina A&T State University, Coltrane Hall 105 B

336 285 4683   cliang@ncat.edu

NOTES

Customer Survey Sample

	Product Concepts				Comments and Suggestions
Clear Product Description	4 (Excellent)	3 (Good)	2 (Satisfactory)	1 (Need Improvement)	
Creativity and Uniqueness	4 (Excellent)	3 (Good)	2 (Satisfactory)	1 (Need Improvement)	
Usefulness	4 (Excellent)	3 (Good)	2 (Satisfactory)	1 (Need Improvement)	
Direct Benefits to Customers	4 (Excellent)	3 (Good)	2 (Satisfactory)	1 (Need Improvement)	
Sales					
Pricing	4 (Very Reasonable)	3 (Acceptable)	2 (Priced Too Low)	1 (Priced Too High)	**Suggested Prices:**
Appealing to Customers	4 (Excellent)	3 (Good)	2 (Satisfactory)	1 (Need Improvement)	
Will Customer Buy?	4 (Very Likely)	3 (Likely)	2 (Maybe)	1 (Not at All)	
Presentation and Professionalism					
Table Presentation	4 (Excellent)	3 (Good)	2 (Satisfactory)	1 (Need Improvement)	
Responding to Customers	4 (Excellent)	3 (Good)	2 (Satisfactory)	1 (Need Improvement)	
Promotion	4 (Excellent)	3 (Good)	2 (Satisfactory)	1 (Need Improvement)	
Teamwork	4 (Excellent)	3 (Good)	2 (Satisfactory)	1 (Need Improvement)	

Create Team Working Schedules (Week 1, 2, 3, 4)

Information Returned to the Instructor

Daily Work Hours by Individuals—Print Your Last Name Clearly by Time

	Monday	Tuesday	Wednesday	Thursday	Friday
8:00 a.m.					
8:15					
8:30					
8:45					
9:00					
9:15					
9:30					
9:45					
10:00					
10:15					
10:30					
10:45					
11:00					
11:15					
11:30					
11:45					

Daily Work Hours by Individuals—Print Your Last Name Clearly by Time

	Monday	Tuesday	Wednesday	Thursday	Friday
12:00 p.m.					
12:15					
12:30					
12:45					
1:00					
1:15					
1:30					
1:45					
2:00					
2:15					
2:30					
2:45					
3:00					
3:15					
3:30					
3:45					
4:00					
4:15					
4:30					
4:45					
5:00 p.m. (close)					

Understand Operation Rules and Prepare for Operating Procedures

STEP 9

To establish a successful enterprise, each team needs to understand and create a Standard Operating Practices.

What is a Standard Operating Practice?

- It is a step-by-step instruction for all team members to follow.
- It helps to make sure all team members understand each step clearly and consistently.
- It helps to eliminate ambiguity and confusion.

How to write a good Standard Operating Practices.

- Provide clear direction and instruction to train each team member **what to do** and **how to do** everything.
- Improve communication through a list of clear instructions.
- Reduce training time when you offer clear instructions.
- Support transition of responsibilities when members need to switch tasks. Be flexible.
- Keep it simple and easy—5–10 steps for each type of work.
- Post team information on Facebook for easy access.
- ***Pay attention to details and daily routine—do not assume anything is "common sense"!***

Categories of Standard Operating Practices:

- Pre-open (30 minutes before you actually open for business) and Post-closing (30 minutes after you clean up and close for business) each day
- Production procedures (using video is a plus)
- Cleaning and storage
- Financial recording and counting

Sample Standard Operating Practices—Pre Opening Daily Procedures

- Go to Room 205, use your code to open the safe, pick up your money bag, lock the safe.
- Bring money bag to Room 207, pick up your key, open the bag, put the key back (do not remove key from Room 207).
- Bring money bag to course manager in Room 102, count money before you start operation.
- Bring money bag and supplies to your location.
- Ready for operation.

Sample Standard Operating Practices—Post Opening Daily Procedures

- Go to see course manager in Room 102, count money.
- Bring money bag to Room 207, pick up your key, lock the bag, put the key back (do not remove key from Room 207).
- On Wednesday, the person closing for business must see Elisa in Room 207 for deposit.
- Bring money bag to Room 205, open safe, put money bag in safe, lock safe.
- Make sure storage room is clean.

Sample Standard Operating Practices—Storage Room Policy

- Keep walkway and hallway clear and clean.
- Mark everything with your team name.
- Put everything inside cabinet or in boxes.
- No overnight food, drink, opened container, or cooking items allowed.
- Cheese, other processed dairy, and perishable items must be stored in refrigerator.
- No bread, other baked goods, dirty cookware, and garbage.

Here is a bad practice, why?

Courtesy of Chyi-lyi (Kathleen) Liang

Sample Standard Operating Practices—Food Preparation

- Use gloves (in storage room) while preparing, cooking, and handling food items.
- Wash hands often.
- Use paper towel to wipe dirty spots.
- Keep tablecloth and service space clean.
- One person handles cooking and food, the other person handles money and cleaning.
- Use Morrill Hall kitchen (inside Dean's office) with respect—take a picture before and after you use the kitchen, and post all pictures on Facebook to prove.
- When should we cook our food items?
- Who will prepare ingredients and complete grocery shopping?
- What do we use to cook and serve food?
- What do we do to protect our own cooks?
- What do we do to protect customers—hot food?
- How do we set up cooking station—arrange appliance, serving items, napkins, ingredients?

Sample Standard Operating Practices—Food Storage

- Put perishable items in refrigerator—use containers or wrap up everything using clean materials.
- No leftover food allowed—must prepare and sell freshly prepared food items every day.
- Do not leave bread in storage room—leave them outside Dr. Liang's office in a basket.
- Here is a good practice, why?

Courtesy of Chyi-lyi (Kathleen) Liang

Sample Standard Operating Practices—Production Procedures

- Step-by-step instruction for training and quality control
- Use video to show
- How do you maintain the quality?
- Where will you buy supplies and ingredients? Include direction.
- Who is going to do different things on each day?
- Post everything on Facebook

Sample Standard Operating Practices—Production Procedures

- Must label all of your supplies, appliance, ingredients, table, chairs, and table clothes.
- Design a clear instruction to teach each member to clean different things.
- Teach each member to keep kitchen clean.
- Teach each member to store everything nicely and safely—everything must be in a plastic box and labelled clearly.
- Do not block walkway and hallway in storage room.

Sample Standard Operating Practices—Financial Recording Procedures

- How to count money
- How to record daily transactions
- How to add and subtract correctly
- Who is in charge of the overall financial record?
- Where are the safe, key to money bag, white financial sheet, and green financial sheet?
- What is our team password to open the safe?

This is a bad practice. Why?

Courtesy of Chyi-lyi (Kathleen) Liang

Arrange Team Training Sessions (mandatory for each individual to participate outside class time, 15 minutes for each session)

STEP 10

Each member of every team must attend training sessions offered by Teaching Assistants. Individual training will take 10–15 minutes to cover:

1. Rooms and location for financial records.
2. Storage room and rules.
3. Kitchen and cleaning rules.
4. Daily check-in and check-out routines.
5. Office managers and financial manager.
6. Supplies, materials, and other existing resources.
7. Refrigerator and rules.

Design Advertising and Promotional Materials (1 day)

Promotion, advertising, and direct selling is to give customers the information they need to make a decision to purchase your products, to compare your products with competitors, and to share information with others who might purchase your products. There are different ways to advertise and to promote your products:

- Poster—direct impacts

Poster must include:

- Name of the business
- Name of the course and the statement
- Names of team members and each person's role in this team (photos will be a plus)
- Purpose of your enterprise
- Daily operating hours and location of your Dollar Enterprise
- Charity organization you will support
- Clear description of your ingredients, materials, and other resources
- Photos, images, pictures of your products including prices for different types of products

- Flyer—distribution
  - Name of the business
  - Name of the course and the statement
  - Names of team members
  - Purpose of your enterprise
  - Daily operating hours and location
  - Charity organization you will support
  - Clear description of your ingredients, materials, and other resources
  - Photos, images, pictures of your products including prices for different types of products
  - Emphasize customer/consumer benefits

- Social media—Facebook, Instagram, Pinterest, Twitter, etc.

Constantly post updates about your products, introduce new products, and share stories and customer comments.

- On-site sampling and coupons—taste and discount for new customers
- Mobile advertising—bring your products to classes, club activities, on-campus events, etc.

Learn Financial Recording and Analysis (1 day)

How to Record Sales, Donations, Expenses, and Total Balance

We only accept cash payment.

To record sales,

- Write down each item sold and the sales amount in cash.

To record donation,

- Write down donation amount in cash clearly as a separate category.

To calculate total earnings,

- Add up all sales and donations at the end of the day, and write the total amounts in the space given in the financial record table.
- *Sales must be separated from donation.*

To record expenses,

- Team members need to go shopping using your own money first.
- Keep all the receipts.
- Record items and amount spent clearly.
- Need to be reimbursed the next day.
- *No receipts, no reimbursement!*

Date_____________

People who open for business
____

Beginning Balance

Product Category and Items	Sales Cash (A1)	Donation Cash (A2)	Total = Sales (A1) + Donation (A2)
Total Earnings			

Expenses Name of student who shopped	Items What you bought	Total amount Must have receipts for reimbursement	Paid or not

Ending Balance of Each Day =

Total Earnings (include sales and donation) – Total Expenses = _____________________

How to Make a Deposit Each Week

At the end of each day, please come to instructor's office to count money and to deposit.

Understand and Create Critical Assumptions, Risks, and Contingency Planning (1 day)

What are critical assumptions and why do we care? Write down your assumptions. You are making assumptions about a lot of things before, during, and after your operation. For example, you will make assumptions with respect to weather, production, inventory, team members, customers, etc.

What are risks and why do we care? There are risks, thinking them through and writing them down clarifies them for your team.

What is contingency planning and why do we care? What if what we have planned doesn't happen? What will we do and what are the consequences?

Prepare for Show-and-Tell (1 day)

Prepare for an Initial Business Plan—Let Us Put Everything Together First (1 day)

STEP 15

Prepare an Initial Business Model

A business model uses a simplified version of a plan or a diagram to describe how a business competes in the market, how the business gathers and uses the resources, what specific methods the business uses to connect with partners and consumers, and how the business creates value-added products and services and leads to sustainability of the business.

There are five basic elements of an effective business model: basic strategy, resources needed, strategic alliances and partnership, customer relation, and communication strategy.

1. Basic strategy—mission, product/service, customers, benefits, value added, and uniqueness.
2. Resources needed—venture competencies (what you are good at) and resources.
3. Strategic alliances and partnership—community partners, suppliers, charity organizations, and other key alliances.
4. Customer relation—target customer, customer satisfaction, customer surveys, reasonable pricing structures, and locations.
5. Communication strategy—communication with the instructor, university officials, team members, customers, community partners, suppliers, charities, and other key alliances.

For each individual in a team, you need to develop a graphic illustration to:

- Show a business model that includes all the required elements *in a drawing.* (The instructor will provide a sample in class.)
- Please include *sufficient narrative explanation* that describes how each required element relates to the others in your model.
- The team will vote on the best business model (drawing and narratives) to be included in the final business report.

A Sample Business Model

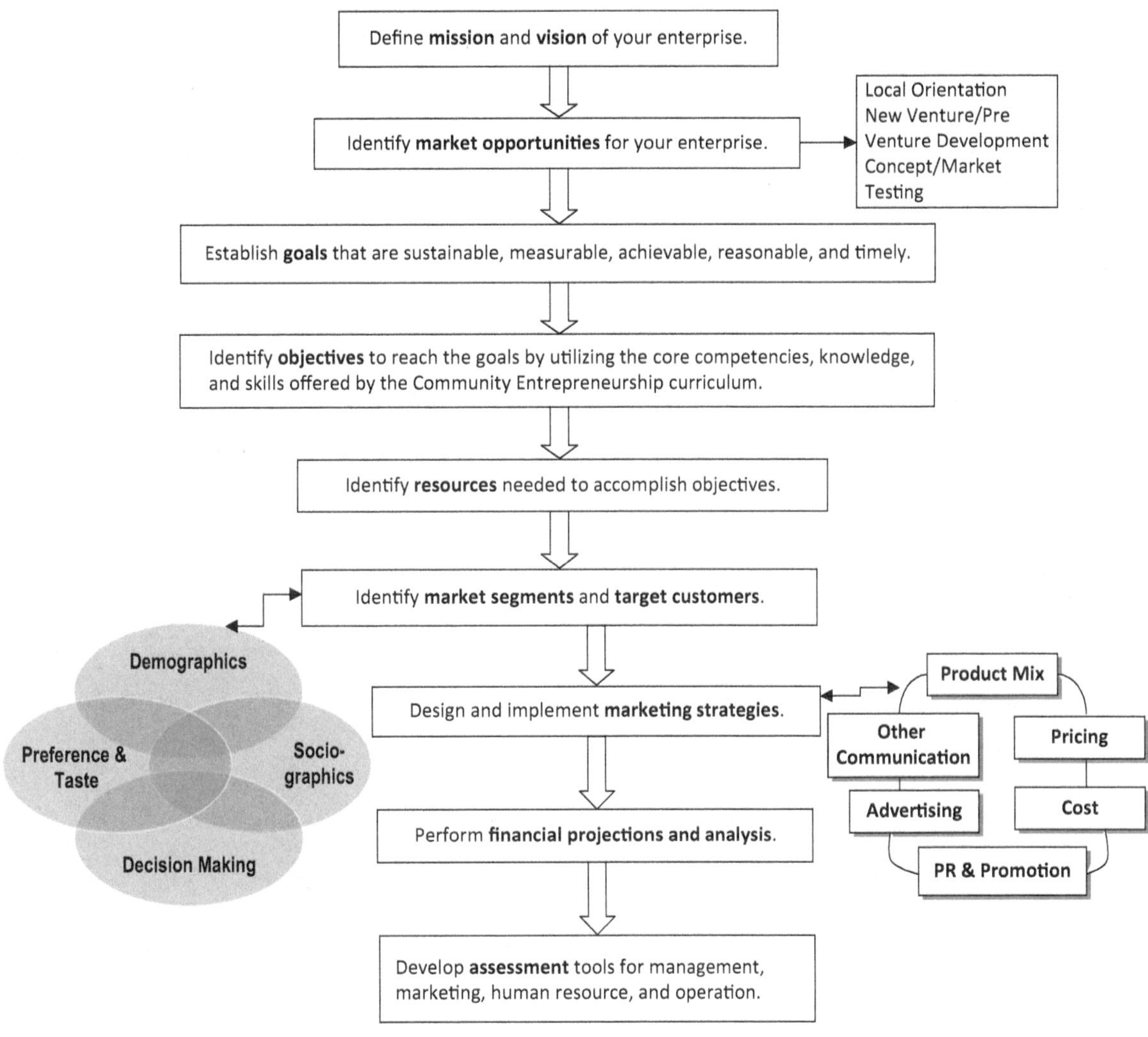

Courtesy of Chyi-lyi (Kathleen) Liang

NOTES

NOTES

NOTES

Writing an Initial Business Plan

Sample Initial Business Plan Outline and Required Contents

Format Requirements

- ❑ Cover page
- ❑ Table of contents (include page numbers)
- ❑ Page numbers (including appendices)
- ❑ Consistent font size and style
- ❑ Spelling and grammar check (use the writing lab in your university library)
- ❑ Section titles are not at the end of the page
- ❑ Graphs have numbers and titles (references if necessary)
- ❑ Tables have numbers and titles (references if necessary)
- ❑ Appendices have titles and page numbers
- ❑ Reference style
- ❑ Append forms, résumé, agreements, licenses, and other legal documents

Package

- ❑ In a binder
- ❑ Samples of advertising and promotion materials
- ❑ Forms
- ❑ Table and Figures

NOTES

NOTES

Contents (This is only a sample. You need to check and modify this for your own business.)

❏ Introduction
- Who you are—list each team member by their roles and responsibilities, describe each individual's experience and background clearly in short paragraphs.
- Concept statement for your product or service.
  A concept statement is to describe products, purpose, target customer, location, sales strategies, and benefits of products. This is one paragraph to summarize who, what, why, how, and expected outcomes.
- What the business idea is—describe your products and services clearly.
- Mission statement—a mission statement is to describe what your business hopes to achieve. You can find many examples of mission statements online. The key is to keep it simple, clear, and easy to understand.
- Goals and objectives (goals are broad and objectives are specific actions to reach your goals).
  For example,
  - Week 1 goal: our goal in the first week is to sell 50 cookies each day.
  - Week 1 objectives: we need to bake 50 cookies each day by 9 a.m. for sale, we need to purchase fresh ingredients 3 times each week, and we need to deliver 50 cookies to campus by 8:30 a.m. every day.
- Describe your charitable organization—include director, mission statement, the functions of this organization, and other notable things that you would like to share.
- Location of your business.
- Financial needs for pre-business preparation (startup)—list all items clearly by quantity and value, including donated items and free items.
- Procedures to start the business (step-by-step details including applying for permits, getting donations, purchasing stuff, etc.) Think about how your team started this Dollar Enterprise process from Day 1 of this course—Dr. Liang applies for permits, brainstorm an idea, organize team members, design product, etc.

❏ Market and marketing
- Campus environment—student distribution, growth, etc. (need to conduct research to find this information)
- Not all campus members are your customers. Think carefully, who are your customers exactly?
  Do they like vegetarian food?
  Do they like to purchase specific kind of jewelry?
  Do they have specific dietary needs?
  What are your customers' hobbies and preferences?
  Do they like certain types of colors, sizes, and design?
- Competitive analysis and SWOT (strengths, weaknesses, opportunities, and threats) analysis This is to compare and contrast your products with other competitors. You can use a table to list each competitor and describe your strength, weakness, opportunities, and threats. For example,

	Strength	**Weakness**	**Opportunities**	**Threats**
Dollar Enterprise cookie team	Donate to charity Local farm ingredients	Must be purchased by cash Only available a few days a week	Promote local connection and support local farms	Dining hall offers the same types of cookies
Campus dining hall cookies	Convenient to purchase Included in campus meal plan, no extra charge	Not appealing to certain types of customers	Improve on quality and varieties	Dollar Enterprise becomes more creative and popular

There are a lot of competitors on campus, you need to create a detailed list!

- Niche—uniqueness of your products and services, usefulness of your products and services, why you believe your products will be popular, etc.
- Target market relationship to your location—describe consumption patterns on campus. Where do people go to purchase similar products? Is your choice of location a wise strategy? Why?
- Target customers—describe customer demographics.
- Describe survey procedures, design of questionnaires, and number of samples, how you propose to conduct surveys, and where you would go to conduct surveys.
- Promotion and advertising strategies, material design, material distribution, and evaluation of effectiveness.
- Pricing strategies—how do you decide your prices? How do you calculate price for each product?

❏ Operations
- Decision-making process—describe your teamwork to make decisions about production, purchasing, inventory management, and daily sales. Describe who is taking the lead in different types of decisions, how you communicate with each other to make decisions, how you resolve conflicts when you are making decisions, etc.
- Procedures to create the product or service—describe step-by-step how you make your stuff, where you ordered the stuff, the process to make or order your stuff, how long it takes to make or receive the orders, etc.
- Daily routine for set-up and selling—work schedules by individuals and set-up, preparation, cleaning, closing, and if you do not sell, then what else will you do?
- Explain your Operating Practices clearly by required category.
- Customer services, satisfaction, evaluation, adjustment, etc.—how do you work with customers to get their feedback for improvement? How do you reward and encourage customers to help you?

❑ Finance
  - Explain clearly how much stuff you will need in the pre-business preparation, initial investment, where resources will come from, etc.
  - Estimated production or services for each day and each week. Provide a table to show daily production, sales, material/ingredient purchase, etc.

❏ Critical assumptions

❏ Risk analysis

❏ Contingency plan

Establish Rules for Peer Assessment and Self-Assessment (4 weeks in operation)

1. The importance of assessment
2. Different approaches to conduct assessment
3. Assessment items
4. Assessment methods
5. Results and communication

Prepare Weekly Reports
(4 weeks in operation)

For Each Member

Peer evaluation will be provided to each student in class. Each member will evaluate team members with respect to work ethic, workload, communication, and professionalism.

For Each Team

Each team will have opportunities to evaluate other teams on our Team Spirit Day. Our class runs Team Spirit Day in each week, often starting on the second week of Dollar Enterprise operation. Team evaluation focuses on product design, creativity, teamwork, customer services, and professionalism.

Part 1. Your own evaluation about <u>your team</u> from the first day of class to now

5 = extremely satisfied   1 = extremely dissatisfied

Team members' attitude in working together	5	4	3	2	1
Team members' willingness to learn entrepreneurial concepts and applications	5	4	3	2	1
Team members' willingness to participate in team meetings in class	5	4	3	2	1
Team members' willingness to participate in team meetings outside class time	5	4	3	2	1
Team members' willingness to contribute to product design and actual production	5	4	3	2	1
Team members' willingness to contribute to writing business plan	5	4	3	2	1
Team members' willingness to contribute to daily operation for Dollar Enterprise since Sept. 28	5	4	3	2	1
Team members' willingness to support each other even when they are not scheduled to sell or to do anything	5	4	3	2	1
Team members' willingness to effectively communicate with others (this is about the whole team, not about a few individuals)	5	4	3	2	1
Team members' willingness to share responsibilities	5	4	3	2	1
Team members' willingness to share ideas and listen to each other	5	4	3	2	1
Team members' willingness to openly discuss issues and solve problems together	5	4	3	2	1
Team members' willingness to accommodate and support each other emotionally	5	4	3	2	1
My team members all have strong work ethic (e.g., show up on time for meetings and table duty, always get things done as assigned and required)	5	4	3	2	1
My team members all have strong professionalism in communication style, respectful language and manner)	5	4	3	2	1
My team policy is very clear and well defined (rewards and consequences)	5	4	3	2	1

Part 2. What I believe my team needs to do to improve

5 = definitely need to improve   1 = don't need any improvement at all

My team needs to communicate more often and more clearly	5	4	3	2	1
My team needs to revise our team policy and make it more reasonable and more clear	5	4	3	2	1
My team needs to be more organized in getting everything done	5	4	3	2	1
My team members need to be more supportive of each other	5	4	3	2	1
My team members need to be more professional in terms of communication style, attitude, and respect	5	4	3	2	1
My team members need to develop stronger work ethic	5	4	3	2	1
My team members need to share workload more evenly	5	4	3	2	1
My team needs to earn more money each day	5	4	3	2	1

Other thoughts about your team to improve? (BONUS)

Part 3. What I expected to learn before I attended Dollar Enterprise **(check all that apply)**

How to write a business plan___
How to start my own business___
What it is like to operate my own business___
What it is like to work with a team___
How to work with a team effectively___
How to communicate with others___
How to prepare for a marketing plan___
How to prepare for financial analysis___
How to make entrepreneurial decisions___

How to make new products___
I did not have any specific expectation___
I was willing to learn everything___
What entrepreneurship is about___
What it is like to be an entrepreneur___
What failure is___
How to transform failure to success___
What resource constraint means___
Others_______________________________________

Part 4. What I have actually learned so far (individual reflection) from the first day of class to now **(check all that apply)**

How to write a business plan___
How to start my own business___
What it is like to operate my own business___
What it is like to work with a team___
How to work with a team effectively___
How to communicate with others___
How to prepare for a marketing plan___
How to prepare for financial analysis___
How to make entrepreneurial decisions___

How to make new products___
I did not have any specific expectation___
I was willing to learn everything___
What entrepreneurship is about___
What it is like to be an entrepreneur___
What failure is___
How to transform failure to success___
What resource constraint means___

Others—BONUS POINTS (Please write in everything else you have learned in this course. Think about what we have covered, and what your team has experienced.)

Prepare for Final Report and Exit Strategy (1 day)

Exit Strategies

When we approach the end of the 4-week operation, each team needs to design exit strategies to close up their operations. To consider exit strategies:

1. Evaluate inventory situation.
2. Evaluate production and sales.
3. Evaluate financial outcomes.

Final report will be prepared using information from

1. Your own plan.
2. Your weekly financial information.
3. Your daily and weekly journals.
4. Peer assessment and reflection.

NOTES

Financial Report

The following table shows an example of financial analysis using the whole class in Fall semester of 2013.

Net Profits = Total Sales – Total Expenses

Ratio 1 = (Total Expenses/Net Profits) × 100

This ratio shows the relationship between total expenses and net profits. It represents the share of the expenses in each dollar of the net profits. The lower this ratio is, the higher efficiency to utilize resources.

Ratio 2 = (Total Expenses/Total Sales) × 100

This ratio shows the relationship between total expenses and total sales. It represents the share of the expenses in each dollar of the total sales. The lower this ratio is, the higher efficiency to utilize resources.

Fall 2013

	Net Profits	Total Expenses	Total Sales	Ratio 1 = (total expenses/net profits) × 100	Ratio 2 = (total expenses/total sales) × 100
pancake	198.87	52.25	251.12	26.27%	20.81%
PuffNStuff	340.53	111.03	451.56	32.61%	24.59%
Jewelry	127.25	13.94	141.19	10.95%	9.87%
sticker	175	0	175	0.00%	0.00%
infinity	282.04	27	309.04	9.57%	8.74%
heady utility	171	25	196	14.62%	12.76%
sustainable style	129.14	15.33	144.47	11.87%	10.61%
trail mix	187.64	88.3	275.94	47.06%	32.00%
breeze	268.54	61.96	330.5	23.07%	18.75%
S'more	117.37	26.6	143.97	22.66%	18.48%
lemonade	156.69	36.14	192.83	23.06%	18.74%
waffle	152	95.41	247.41	62.77%	38.56%
chocolate	192.4	99.1	291.5	51.51%	34.00%
total	2498.47	652.06	3150.53		

Note:

Food related products: Pancake, PuffNStuff (Croissant), Trail Mix, Breeze (grilled cheese sandwich), S'more, Lemonade, Waffle, and Chocolate covered/mix products.

Arts and Crafts related products: Jewelry, Sticker, Infinity (scarf, hair accessories), Heady Utility (utility wears), and Sustainable Style (purse, box, others)

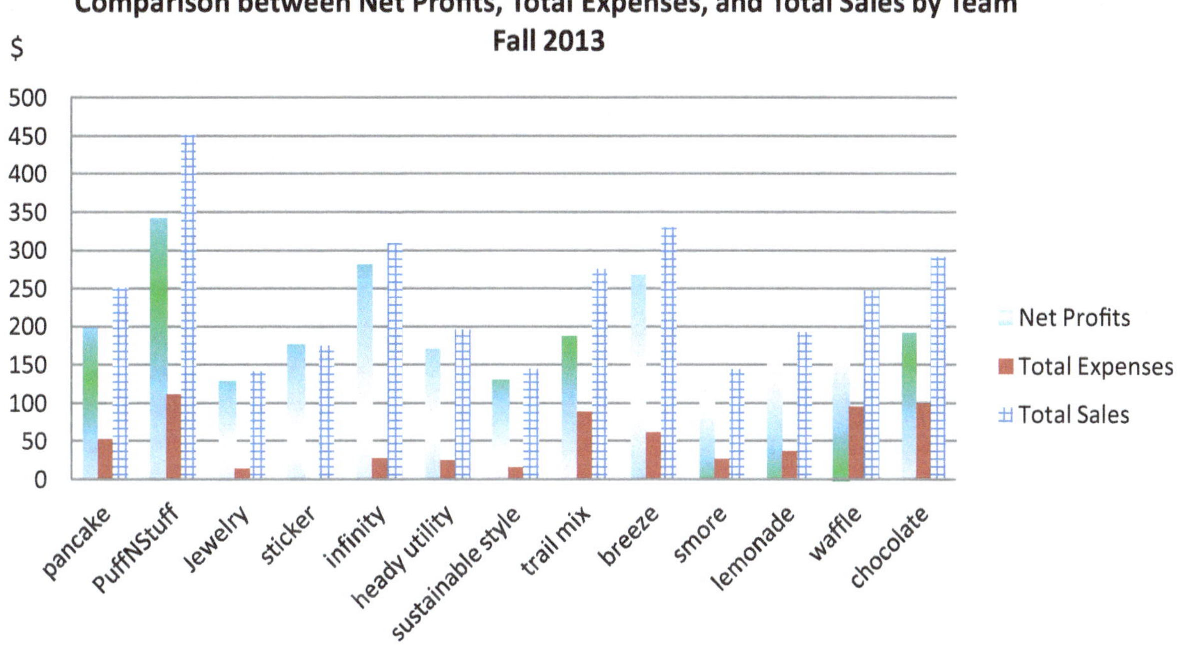

Courtesy of Chyi-lyi (Kathleen) Liang

This graph shows differences in net profits, total expenses, and total sales by teams. PuffNStuff had the highest total sales, and the highest total expenses due to the nature of a food business. Breeze (grilled cheese) and chocolate covered products were also very popular. These two teams had good sales records, however, their total expenses were also higher than other teams. S'more team had the lowest net profits among all food-related businesses, but their total expenses were not as high.

Among non-food businesses, infinity team had the highest net profits, and their total expenses were very reasonable by using recyclable materials. Sticker team had no expenses, because this team received in-kind donation to cover printing expenses from a local vendor. Generally speaking arts and crafts teams had much lower expenses than food businesses by utilizing recyclable and re-usable materials.

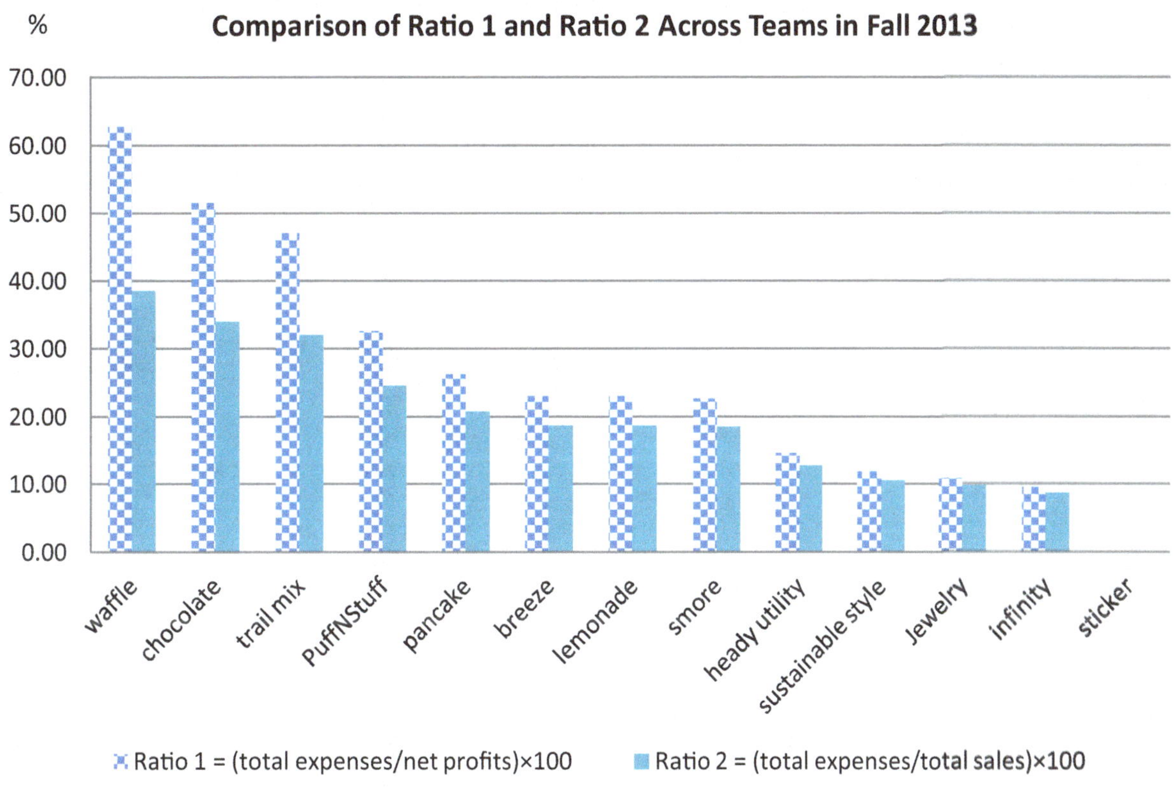

Courtesy of Chyi-lyi (Kathleen) Liang

The ratios show efficiency of resource utilization for each team. Waffle team had the highest ratios. Waffle team spent a lot of money in purchasing ingredients. However their total sales were low. Much of the ingredients could be wasted. It is reasonable to see food-related businesses had lower efficiency ratios than arts/crafts teams. Food ingredients are relatively expensive. Teams must prepare for fresh food and drink items on daily basis, and no overnight products are allowed. Arts and crafts teams are able to utilize recyclable, re-usable materials to create new products. Therefore arts and crafts teams are expected to have lower expenses and higher returns on investment.

Business Experience

Reflection of what you expected to learn, what you actually learned, and how each individual achieved goals.

Team Experience

- Collaboration
- Discrepancies
- Communication

Individual Experience

Final Report

Complete Dollar Enterprise Donation, Overall Assessment, and Overall Reflection

What if we can do this again?

APPENDIX

ENTREPRENEURIAL PROFILE, CHARACTERISTICS, EXPECTATIONS, AND OUTCOMES—AN EMPIRICAL STUDY TO COMPARE RURAL ENTREPRENEURS WITH URBAN ENTREPRENEURS

Chyi-lyi (Kathleen) Liang
The University of Vermont

Paul Dunn
The University of Louisiana at Monroe

Abstract

Policy should be based on good information about the people impacted by the policy. Since rural entrepreneurship development policy has been discussed in rural community development, it would be important to determine if and to what extent rural entrepreneurs are different. This study was designed with that in mind. We discovered that, in general, rural and urban entrepreneurs were very similar with respect to characteristics, decision making path, and expectation. However a few significant differences were revealed by our survey. For example, urban entrepreneurs seem a little more optimistic and realistic than rural entrepreneurs in the process of new venture formation. Urban entrepreneurs also were more likely to believe that starting new ventures improved their personal and family's quality of life. In general, policy development should take into consideration some differences between rural and urban populations and community settings. Access to information, education, opportunities, and capital might be issues for rural entrepreneurs more often than for urban entrepreneurs.

Keywords

rural, urban, entrepreneurial characteristics, entrepreneurial decisions

JEL Codes

D2, D7, M2

Acknowledgment

The author is grateful to the funding supported by the USDA NIFA AFRI program grant number 2011-67023-30106 and the USDA Hatch Grant 2011–2014 for conducting research with respect to rural entrepreneurship.

Introduction

Entrepreneurship researchers seem to agree that entrepreneurs recognize and exploit emerging business opportunities through new venture creation (Allen, 1995; Ardichhvili, Cardozo, & Ray, 1993). Many also recognize that entrepreneurs in creating new ventures add employment, income, wealth and quality of life to their communities. The impacts of entrepreneurial actions and decisions have been clearly documented and reported, however most of the discussions focus on job creation and wealth, distributions in urban areas or high-population density regions associated with intensive technology innovations. Rural communities face different challenges compared to urban areas. Shortage of skilled and qualified labor, lack of investment incentives, and limited resources and opportunities often threaten entrepreneurial decisions in new venture creation and economic development. Rural developers who have followed the traditional industry attraction strategy have realized that entrepreneurs and entrepreneurship may offer an alternative approach, grow your own, to develop their communities. Many issues need to be examined before establishing frameworks to design, promote, and encourage rural entrepreneurship, such as (1) are there any significant differences between rural entrepreneurs and urban entrepreneurs? (2) do urban or rural locations make any differences for entrepreneurs in the pursuit of their own opportunities in new venture creation? and (3) do urban and rural entrepreneurs assess their expectations and outcomes the same way in venture formation process?

The focus of this paper is to introduce an empirical study using survey data collected from both rural and urban entrepreneurs. The purpose of this study is to discover if and to what extent rural entrepreneurs differ from their urban counterparts with respect to characteristics, and expectations/outcomes associated with new venture decision. We believe that it would be essential to study rural/urban entrepreneurs' expectations, their characteristics, the challenges and barriers of new venture formation, and the outcomes and impacts of starting a new venture on individuals and their families. First, much of the research on rural entrepreneurship has focused on the institutional structures and environment, and how, policy can be established or changed to foster entrepreneurial development. There is limited discussion about how rural entrepreneurs and urban entrepreneurs might be different given their endowed nature of being entrepreneurs. Secondly, it may be instructive to discover if rural entrepreneurs are really different from urban entrepreneurs with respect to individual decision-making process and entrepreneurial mindset before establishing rural development strategies and policies. Finally, little research has been devoted to discovering if rural entrepreneurs are different from entrepreneurs generally or from urban entrepreneurs specifically prior to or after new venture formation, how their mindset might be changed in the process of new venture creation, and any impacts of new venture creation on their families.

Literature Review

Research on entrepreneurial characteristics generally has discussed high achievement drive, action oriented, internal locus of control, tolerance for ambiguity, moderate risk taking, commitment, opportunistic, initiative, independence, commitment/tenacity, creativity, and optimism (Liang & Dunn, 2003; Malach-Pines, Sadeh, Dvir, & Yafe-Yanai, 2002; Crane & Sohl, 2004; Liang & Dunn, 2008). Many scholars have attempted to design and create conceptual frameworks that would generalize entrepreneurial individuals' traits and profile. There is still no conclusive discussion with respect to who entrepreneurs are and what entrepreneurs are like. Some have argued that it would not be appropriate to solely examine who entrepreneurs were, since entrepreneurial individuals were influenced by a combination of social, economic, and environmental induction (Sarasvathy, 2003).

Several researchers have discussed the role of optimism as a motive force accounting for persistence and commitment (Kuratko & Hodgetts, 2004; Litt, Tennen, Affleck, & Klock, 1992; Seligman & Schulman, 1986; McColl-Kennedy & Anderson, 2005; Liang & Dunn, 2008; Liang & Dunn, 2011). Optimism has also been seen as a negative force among entrepreneurs resulting in their tendency to create ventures with a high risk of failure (Baron & Shane, 2005; Hey, 1984; Petrakis, 2005; De Meza & Southey, 1996; Coelho & De Meza, 2006; Brocas & Carrillo, 2004; Puri & Robinson, 2004; Simon & Houghton, 2002;

Hmielski & Baron, 2009). Optimism as it is discussed in entrepreneurship research and literature is similar to "dispositional optimism" in psychology, which represents biases held, across time and situations, positive expectations (Sujan, 1999; Wrosch & Scheier, 2003; Chang, 2001; Crane & Crane, 2007; Haugen, Ommundsen & Lund, 2004). Psychology research and literature indicates that optimists feel in control of their activities, their activities will give them more satisfaction, they initiate projects, they feel they have the time to carry them out, have made progress toward their goal, and have heightened expectations that their project outcomes will be successful and will therefore yield more positive outcomes in well-being and coping behavior (Jackson, Weiss, Lundquist & Soderlind, 2002; Leung, Moneta & McBrice-Chang, 2005; Day & Maltby, 2003; Wrosch & Sheier, 2003; Scheier & Carver, 1987). Recent studies have discovered differentiating factors to compare entrepreneurial optimism, realism, and pessimism using empirical data gathered from entrepreneurs (Manove, 2000; Liang & Dunn, 2008; Liang & Dunn, 2011). The new findings led to deeper understanding of different impacts of optimism, realism, and pessimism on entrepreneurial decision making.

Fraser and Greene (2006) in developing an occupational choice model have suggested that entrepreneurs learn from experience and that both optimistic bias and uncertainty go down with experience--that suggests that the more entrepreneurs learn, the more realistic they become. A few entrepreneurship scholars have discussed relationship between entrepreneurial traits, business opportunity recognition, new venture performance, and positive expectations for entrepreneurs (Shane & Venkataraman, 2000). Entrepreneurial learning may occur at any point prior to, or during the new venture planning and formation process. Entrepreneurs learn from their existing work experiences, family interactions, or networking connections (Liang & Dunn, 2012). Entrepreneurs who have started multiple new ventures seem to learn more from failure.

The field of entrepreneurship has included studies of entrepreneurial individuals, entrepreneurial environment, entrepreneurial triggers, and entrepreneurial incentives. There has been very limited discussion about rural entrepreneurs versus urban entrepreneurs. Given the pressure of rural development in the United States, it is critical to explore how rural entrepreneurs perceive opportunities, challenges, and expectations. It is often assumed that entrepreneurs engage in new venture creation for profit. In contrast to this view, this paper argues that entrepreneurship is more adequately characterized as a self-satisfying activity. New venture creation seems rewarding because it provides substantial non-monetary benefits, such as greater autonomy, broader skill utilization, and the possibility to pursue one's own ideas, which are critical for rural development.

Methods

Survey Design

The first step of our research was to design a questionnaire. The target respondents to this survey were in-business entrepreneurs. The survey questions included: demographics of the entrepreneur and the business, optimism/realism assessment, expectations, and personal and business outcomes from the venture.

Entrepreneurial and business demographics included gender, age, ethnicity, marital status, education, entrepreneur's experience, type of business, location of the business and number of full-time and part-time employees. Entrepreneurial characteristics included in this study were independence, taking control, believing they were creative and being willing to accept risks. The answers were on a Likert scale as Strongly Agree (1), Agree (2), Disagree (3), and Strongly Disagree (4). We avoided the "Neither Agree or Disagree" level and hoped to impose more specific choices on entrepreneurs.

Optimism assessment statements were adopted from the Life Orientation Test (LOT-R) which contains three positive statements, three negative statements, and four non-scored items as filler statements. Three positive statements were: "In uncertain times, I usually expect the best," "I am always optimistic about my future," "Overall I always expect more good things happen to me than bad." Three negative statements were: "If something can go wrong for me, it will." "I hardly ever expect things to go my

way," and "I rarely count on good things happening to me." The LOT-R test is recognized and used by psychologists as a sufficient and robust tool to measure optimism. The LOT-R has been used to explore personal control in sports, to investigate the relationship between optimism and depression/coping/anger, to analyze effects of optimism on career choice and well-being, and to examine the impact of optimism on changes of environment and circumstantial situations (Burke et al., 2006; Burke, Joyner, Czech & Wilson, 2000; Puskar, Sereika, Lamb, Tusaie-Mumford, & Mcguinness, 1999; Creed, Patton & Bertram, 2002; Perczek, Carver, Price, & Pozo-Kaderman, 2000; Sydney et al., 2005). Clinical researchers have used the LOT-R to explore how optimism affects patients in dealing with health problems and therapies (Walker, Nail, Larsen, Magill, & Schwartz, 1996). The LOT-R is available on-line and it is free for researchers to use (Centre for Confidence and Well-being, 2006). There are 5 levels of choices in the original LOT-R test, which are I Agree a Lot (1), I Agree a Little (2), I Neither Agree Nor Disagree (3), I Disagree a Little (4), and I Disagree a Lot (5).

There is no research-based instrument to measure *realism* in the literature. We generated a list of realism statement, conducted a thorough literature review in psychological and entrepreneurial research, and extensive discussions and consultations with entrepreneurs and entrepreneurship educators. The seven realism statements were: "I usually set achievable goals," "I usually look before I leap," "When planning, I usually consider both negative and positive outcomes," "I am always realistic about my future," "I try to be reasonably certain about the situation I face when starting an important activity," and "I usually weigh the risks and rewards when making decisions." Entrepreneurs responded based on a five-point Likert scale ranging from "I agree a lot" to "I disagree a lot," which was the same scale used in LOT-R testing optimism statements.

Expectations and outcomes questions asked entrepreneurs to identify levels of satisfaction prior to and after starting new ventures. Questions included reflections of personal happiness, personal financial satisfaction, family happiness, family financial satisfaction, and impacts on marriage if survey respondents are married. There are 5 levels of choices to each statement, which are I Agree a Lot (1), I Agree a Little (2), I Neither Agree Nor Disagree (3), I Disagree a Little (4), and I Disagree a Lot (5).

Survey Procedure

The questionnaire was pre-tested among researchers and entrepreneurs and administered to business entrepreneurs by a research contact person. Only entrepreneurs were asked to respond to the survey, not including their spouses and children to avoid conflict of interests. Therefore the answers only reflect entrepreneurs' own perceptions. The entrepreneur was given the questionnaire (delivered to their business addresses) and allowed to complete it in private during business hours or another convenient time for the business owner and returned it. The questionnaire was administered to a convenience sample of business owners in the Mississippi River Delta region between 2007 and 2011. There were 564 respondents totally.

Statistical Analysis

Cross tabulations were performed and two statistics, Chi square and Gamma were calculated to determine if there were significant differences between rural and urban entrepreneurs in the study.

Results

Findings of the study are summarized in the following tables. Table 1 shows that with respect to gender, ethnicity, and age, rural and urban entrepreneurs were very similar. Approximately 2/3 of both groups were male, 80 percent were white, and the majority was over 30 years of age. Education levels among urban entrepreneurs were significantly higher than among rural entrepreneurs. On the other hand, significantly more of rural entrepreneurs were married while more of urban entrepreneurs were single. Entrepreneurial characteristics (Table 2) including being independent, control, creative, and risk taking were similar in both urban and rural groups with 90+ percent agreeing or strongly agreeing that they had these characteristics.

Table 1—Survey Respondents' Demographics					
Gender	**Rural**	**Urban**	**Education**	**Rural**	**Urban**
Female	33.2%	35.4%	Less than high school	4.1%	2.5%
Male	66.8%	64.6%	High School	35.9%	18.9%
Total	100.0%	100.0%	Some College	27.2%	35.9%
N	232	311	College Degree	27.2%	34.5%
Chi Square	0.331		Graduate Degree	5.5%	8.2%
Gamma	0.596		Total	100.0%	100.0%
Ethnicity			N	217	281
White	84.1%	77.0%	Chi Square	0.000***	
African American	13.4%	17.6%	Gamma	0.000***	
Asian	2.2%	2.6%	**Marital Status**		
Hispanic	0.0%	1.9%	Single	10.8%	18.6%
American Indian	.4%	.6%	Single/children	16.4%	11.5%
Other	0.0%	.3%	Married/children	68.5%	63.5%
Total	100.0%	100.0%	Married w/o children	4.3%	6.4%
N	232	313	Total	100.0%	100.0%
Chi Square	0.173		N	232	312
Gamma	0.029*		Chi Square	0.027*	
Age			Gamma	0.453	
Under 30 years old	12.8%	16.3%			
30–50 years old	49.8%	47.4%			
Over 50	37.4%	36.3%			
Total	100.0%	100.0%			
N	227	306			
Chi Square	0.517				
Gamma	0.479				
Note: * significant at 0.1, ** significant at 0.01, *** significant at 0.001					

Table 2—Entrepreneurs' Characteristics						
Want Independence			**I am Creative**			
	Rural	**Urban**		**Rural**	**Urban**	
Strongly Agree	67.7%	69.1%	Strongly Agree	44.6%	47.4%	
Agree	27.2%	27.7%	Agree	46.3%	44.2%	
Disagree	3.4%	3.2%	Disagree	7.8%	8.3%	
Strongly Disagree	1.7%	0.0%	Strongly Disagree	1.3%	0.0%	
Total	100.0%	100.0%	Total	100.0%	100.0%	
N	232	314	N	231	312	
Chi Square	0.139		Chi Square	0.216		
Gamma	0.613		Gamma	0.489		
Want to be in Control			**I Accept Risk**			
strongly agree	71.1%	64.6%	Strongly Agree	65.4%	68.7%	
Agree	25.0%	30.5%	Agree	30.3%	30.0%	
Disagree	2.6%	4.5%	Disagree	3.5%	1.3%	
Strongly Disagree	1.3%	.3%	Strongly Disagree	.9%	0.0%	
Total	100.0%	100.0%	Total	100.0%	100.0%	
N	232	311	N	231	313	
Chi Square	0.151		Chi Square	0.121		
Gamma	0.112		Gamma	0.303		
Note: *significant at 0.1, ** significant at 0.01, *** significant at 0.001						

With respect to experience (Table 3) nearly two-thirds of rural and urban entrepreneurs responding indicated that they had had experience in this line of work before. Over half of both groups responding said they had operational experience before starting the business and over 70 percent indicated that they had managerial experience before starting this business. There were no significant differences between rural and urban entrepreneurs. It should be noted that there was a substantial no response on managerial experience. The business types (Table 4) were similar with slightly more urban than rural service businesses. While there was no statistically significant difference between the number of full-time and part-time employees, rural businesses tended to be a little smaller than urban businesses.

Table 3—Entrepreneurs' Experience		
Line Experience		
	Rural	**Urban**
Yes	63.2%	64.4%
No	36.8%	35.6%
Total	100.0%	100.0%
N	228	309
Chi Square	0.418	
Gamma	0.767	
Operation Experience		
0–5	51.6%	54.1%
6–10	19.0%	20.6%
11+	22.2%	20.1%
None	7.2%	5.3%
Total	100.0%	100.0%
N	153	209
Chi Square	0.815	
Gamma	0.483	
Management Experience		
1–5	34.8%	30.1%
6–10	16.9%	23.8%
11+	31.5%	37.1%
None	16.9%	9.1%
Total	100.0%	100.0%
N	89	143
Chi Square	0.182	
Gamma	0.304	
Note: *significant at 0.1, ** significant at 0.01, *** significant at 0.001		

Table 4—Business Demographics		
Type of Business	**Rural**	**Urban**
Retail	32.6%	29.4%
Service	50.4%	58.8%
Distribution	4.3%	0.0%
Contractor	0.0%	1.3%
Other	7.4%	6.7%
Manufacturer	5.2%	3.8%
Total	100.0%	100.0%
N	230	313
Chi Square	0.002**	
Gamma	0.912	
Full-time Employees		
0–5	75.1%	67.9%
6–10	11.8%	13.5%
11 and Over	10.0%	16.4%
None	3.2%	2.2%
Total	100.0%	100.0%
N	221	274
Chi Square	0.144	
Gamma	0.074*	
Part-time Employees		
0–5	74.7%	68.7%
6–10	6.5%	8.4%
11 and Over	4.3%	13.2%
None	14.5%	9.7%
Total	100.0%	100.0%
N	186	227
Chi Square	0.008**	
Gamma	0.332	
Note: * significant at 0.1, ** significant at 0.01, *** significant at 0.001		

The measures of optimist/pessimism (Table 5), important indicators of an entrepreneurial orientation, showed no difference between rural and urban entrepreneurs on "expect the best" and "always optimistic" (optimism measures), and "whatever can go wrong will" and "rarely count on good things" (pessimism measures). In general both rural and urban entrepreneurs seemed to be optimistic, over 70 percent agree with the measures, than pessimistic however, around 20 percent agree with the measures. Interestingly, on one measure of optimism, expect more good than bad, urban entrepreneurs were more supportive to this statement. On one measure of pessimism, don't expect things to go my way, rural entrepreneurs were more likely to support this statement.

Table 5—Entrepreneurial Optimism/Pessimism						
Optimism				**Pessimism**		
Expect the Best				**Whatever Can Go Wrong Will**		
	Rural	**Urban**			**Rural**	**Urban**
Agree a Lot	37.7%	42.3%		Agree a Lot	10.8%	8.4%
Agree	36.4%	35.5%		Agree	14.7%	14.0%
Neither	16.5%	15.5%		Neither	29.0%	23.1%
Disagree	8.2%	5.8%		Disagree	24.7%	26.0%
Disagree a Lot	1.3%	1.0%		Disagree a Lot	20.8%	28.6%
Total	100.0%	100.0%		Total	100.0%	100.0%
N	231	310		N	231	308
Chi Square	0.724			Chi Square	0.204	
Gamma	0.198			Gamma	0.032*	
Always Optimistic				**Don't Expect Things to Go My Way**		
Agree a Lot	47.4%	50.3%		Agree a Lot	3.5%	8.7%
Agree	34.5%	34.6%		Agree	15.7%	8.4%
Neither	12.1%	9.8%		Neither	20.5%	15.8%
Disagree	5.2%	4.6%		Disagree	27.9%	22.6%
Disagree a Lot	.9%	.7%		Disagree a Lot	32.3%	44.5%
Total	100.0%	100.0%			100.0%	100.0%
N	232	306			229	310
Chi Square	0.905			Chi Square	0.001***	
Gamma	0.390			Gamma	0.029*	
Expect More Good Than Bad				**Rarely Count on Good Things**		
Agree a Lot	47.0%	60.9%		Agree a Lot	8.2%	8.7%
Agree	39.2%	28.6%		Agree	14.7%	11.3%
Neither	9.9%	6.3%		Neither	18.6%	15.2%
Disagree	2.6%	2.0%		Disagree	29.9%	25.6%
Disagree a Lot	1.3%	2.3%		Disagree a Lot	28.6%	39.2%
Total	100.0%	100.0%		Total	100.0%	100.0%
N	232	304		N	231	309
Chi Square	0.015*			Chi Square	0.120	
Gamma	0.003**			Gamma	0.036*	
Note: * significant at 0.1, ** significant at 0.01, *** significant at 0.001						

Another important measure of an entrepreneurial orientation is realism (Table 6). Both rural and urban entrepreneurs similarly set achievable goals, looked before they leap, considered negative and positive outcomes, weighed risks and rewards, and tried to be certain about the future. More than 75 percent of both groups either agreed or strongly agreed with these assertions. Rural and urban entrepreneurs differed statistically significantly on realism statements about the future with urban entrepreneurs slightly more realistic.

Table 6—Entrepreneurial Realism						
Set Achievable Goals				**Realistic About the Future**		
	Rural	**Urban**			**Rural**	**Urban**
Agree a Lot	56.0%	62.7%		Agree a Lot	40.1%	53.1%
Agree	32.8%	30.9%		Agree	44.8%	31.2%
Neither	6.5%	4.5%		Neither	11.2%	10.9%
Disagree	3.4%	1.9%		Disagree	1.3%	3.9%
Disagree a Lot	1.3%	0.0%		Disagree a Lot	2.6%	1.0%
Total	100.0%	100.0%		Total	100.0%	100.0%
N	232	311		N	232	311
Chi Square	0.121			Chi Square	0.002**	
Gamma	0.063*			Gamma	0.020*	
Look Before I Leap				**Weigh Risks and Rewards**		
Agree a Lot	45.0%	51.6%		Agree a Lot	48.7%	57.5%
Agree	31.6%	31.6%		Agree	35.7%	32.1%
Neither	12.1%	8.1%		Neither	9.1%	6.7%
Disagree	6.9%	7.1%		Disagree	4.3%	3.0%
Disagree a Lot	4.3%	1.6%		Disagree a Lot	2.2%	.7%
Total	100.0%	100.0%		Total	100.0%	100.0%
N	231	310		N	230	299
Chi Square	0.140			Chi Square	0.182	
Gamma	0.060*			Gamma	0.024*	
Consider Negative and Positive Outcomes				**Try to Be Certain About Situation**		
Agree a Lot	55.6%	62.8%		Agree a Lot	50.9%	59.0%
Agree	29.3%	27.8%		Agree	37.0%	33.6%
Neither	9.1%	4.9%		Neither	8.3%	6.5%
Disagree	3.9%	3.9%		Disagree	2.6%	.7%
Disagree a Lot	2.2%	.6%		Disagree a Lot	1.3%	.3%
Total	100.0%	100.0%		Total	100.0%	100.0%
N	232	309		N	230	307
Chi Square	0.132			Chi Square	0.107	
Gamma	0.052*			Gamma	0.032*	
Find Information Before Deciding						
Agree a Lot	46.9%	60.6%				
Agree	38.2%	27.0%				
Neither	7.5%	7.2%				
Disagree	4.4%	4.2%				
Disagree a Lot	3.1%	1.0%				
Total	100.0%	100.0%				
N	228	307				
Chi Square	0.013*					
Gamma	0.003**					
Note: * significant at 0.1, ** significant at 0.01, *** significant at 0.001						

Entrepreneurial expectations are an important measure of their enterprise view (Table 7). Both rural and urban entrepreneurs expected that starting the business would make them happier and expected their families to be happier, over 60 percent. Rural and urban entrepreneurs expected starting a business would make them better off, over 70 percent. Urban entrepreneurs had statistically significantly higher expectations, 71 percent, versus rural, 68 percent, that the business would make their families feel better off. This may indicate some friction in the family.

Table 7—Expectations of New Venture Creation						
Expected to Be Happier				**Expected to Be Better Off**		
	Rural	**Urban**			**Rural**	**Urban**
Strongly Agree	26.1%	28.1%		Strongly Agree	36.5%	35.8%
Agree	35.7%	42.5%		Agree	38.7%	38.7%
Disagree	27.0%	22.7%		Disagree	15.7%	20.1%
Strongly Disagree	11.3%	6.7%		Strongly Disagree	9.1%	5.4%
Total	100.0%	100.0%		Total	100.0%	100.0%
N	230	313		N	230	313
Chi Square	0.112			Chi Square	0.254	
Gamma	0.074*			Gamma	0.990	
Expected Family to Be Happier				**Family Expected to Be Better Off**		
Strongly Agree	25.1%	26.8%		Strongly Agree	27.4%	28.3%
Agree	34.8%	41.9%		Agree	40.7%	43.3%
Disagree	26.4%	24.2%		Disagree	23.0%	22.7%
Strongly Disagree	13.7%	7.0%		Strongly Disagree	8.8%	5.7%
Total	100.0%	100.0%		Total	100.0%	100.0%
N	227	298		N	226	300
Chi Square	0.550			Chi Square	0.052*	
Gamma	0.442			Gamma	0.074*	
Note: * significant at 0.1, ** significant at 0.01, *** significant at 0.001						

In assessing business outcomes (Table 8), rural and urban entrepreneurs agreed that their sales and profits were at or above expectations, over 90 percent. Actual reported sales were slightly lower among rural entrepreneurs' businesses. Over 90 percent of both groups indicated that their businesses were up and running well. Understanding new venture creation process is always a challenge for many people, although earning profits might not be the sole reason for starting own ventures. Many entrepreneurs decide to plan and start their own businesses without any experiences or gathering sufficient information. Over 60 percent of rural and urban entrepreneurs thought that starting their business was harder than expected and over 45 percent thought that it took longer to start than expected (Table 9). These statistics may be instructive for consultants to use with "wanna-bes."

Table 8—Business Outcomes						
Sales Compared With Expectations				**Profit Compared With Expectations**		
	Rural	**Urban**			**Rural**	**Urban**
Higher	37.3%	38.2%		Higher	33.5%	33.0%
About	53.5%	54.4%		About	48.0%	53.1%
Lower	9.2%	7.4%		Lower	18.5%	13.9%
Total	100.0%	100.0%		Total	100.0%	100.0%
N	228	309		N	227	309
Chi Square	0.761			Chi Square	0.301	
Gamma	0.667			Gamma	0.565	
Annual Sales				**Business Up and Running Well**		
Less than $500,000	70.1%	63.6%		Strongly Agree	55.8%	56.7%
$500,000–1,000,000	16.1%	19.4%		Agree	36.8%	39.5%
1,000,000 +	13.7%	17.0%		Disagree	4.3%	3.8%
Total	100.0%	100.0%		Strongly Disagree	3.0%	0.0%
N	211	294		Total	100.0%	100.0%
Chi Square	0.308			N	231	314
Gamma	0.125			Chi Square	0.020*	
				Gamma	0.577	
Note: * significant at 0.1, ** significant at 0.01, *** significant at 0.001						

Table 9—Length and Difficulty in Starting						
Starting Harder Than Expected				**Starting Took Longer Than Expected**		
	Rural	**Urban**			**Rural**	**Urban**
Strongly Agree	23.8%	21.6%		Strongly Agree	18.3%	17.1%
Agree	37.2%	40.0%		Agree	31.7%	303%
Disagree	32.9%	34.2%		Disagree	38.3%	45.5%
Strongly Disagree	6.1%	4.2%		Strongly Disagree	11.7%	7.1%
Total	100.0%	100.0%		Total	100.0%	100.0%
N	231	310		N	230	310
Chi Square	0.674			Chi Square	0.176	
Gamma	0.965			Gamma	0.989	
Note: * significant at 0.1, ** significant at 0.01, *** significant at 0.001						

In view of their expectations discussed earlier, both rural and urban entrepreneurs reported that they and their families were happier as a result of starting the business (Table 10). Over 80 percent of rural and urban entrepreneurs felt happier and thought that their families were happier. Over 90 percent of rural and urban entrepreneurs felt that they were better off for having started the business. Only 78 percent of rural and 83 percent of urban entrepreneurs thought that their families felt better off. There were no significant differences between the two groups.

Table 10—Happiness and Better Off							
I Am Happier				**Spouse Happier**			
	Rural	**Urban**			**Rural**	**Urban**	
Strongly Agree	37.0%	41.0%		Strongly Agree	29.5%	32.4%	
Agree	47.0%	49.4%		Agree	50.7%	51.9%	
Disagree	14.3%	7.7%		Disagree	16.1%	11.9%	
Strongly Disagree	1.7%	1.9%		Strongly Disagree	3.7%	3.8%	
Total	100.0%	100.0%		Total	100.0%	100.0%	
N	230	310		N	217	293	
Chi Square	0.103			Chi Square	0.579		
Gamma	0.113			Gamma	0.281		
I Am Better Off				**Spouse Feels Better Off**			
Strongly Agree	43.4%	45.0%		Strongly Agree	36.8%	43.3%	
Agree	38.2%	42.4%		Agree	40.2%	39.9%	
Disagree	16.7%	10.3%		Disagree	17.6%	14.2%	
Strongly Disagree	1.8%	2.3%		Strongly Disagree	5.4%	2.6%	
Total	100.0%	100.0%		Total	100.0%	100.0%	
N	228	311		N	204	268	
Chi Square	0.176			Chi Square	0.216		
Gamma	0.341			Gamma	0.063*		
Note: * significant at 0.1, ** significant at 0.01, *** significant at 0.001							

When reality kicks in, entrepreneurs seem to have a different appreciation of the new venture process. Many learned valuable lessons after starting and operating their own businesses (Table 11). Majority respondents were willing to start another new venture, and they believed that their family would support them in the process again. Statistically more urban entrepreneurs were willing to start again and felt their families would support them.

Table 11—Future Decisions		
I Would Start Again		
	Rural	**Urban**
Strongly Agree	53.9%	62.8%
Agree	34.3%	30.7%
Disagree	8.7%	4.9%
Strongly Disagree	3.0%	1.3%
Not Sure	0.0%	.3%
Total	100.0%	100.0%
N	230	309
Chi Square	0.091*	
Gamma	0.020*	
Family Would Support Me Again		
Strongly Agree	46.4%	56.4%
Agree	36.2%	32.3%
Disagree	13.8%	8.2%
Strongly Disagree	3.6%	2.4%
Not Sure	0.0%	.7%
Total	100.0%	100.0%
N	224	291
Chi Square	0.067*	
Gamma	0.015*	
Note: * significant at 0.1, ** significant at 0.01, *** significant at 0.001		

Many scholars have discussed new venture creation and its effect on marriage (Aldrich & Cliff, 2003; Bruce, 1999; Bures et al., 1996; King, 1998; Liang & Dunn, 2013; Lieberman, 2000). While not statistically significant, a substantial number of rural entrepreneurs (almost 30 percent) and urban entrepreneurs (28 percent) experienced a negative impact on their marriages in the new venture creation process (Table 12). Single individuals were not expected to respond to this last question. Literature showed both positive and negative influences of business start-up on marriage and family relationships (Liang & Dunn, 2013). In our sample, 20–22 percent of the respondents agreed that their marriage situation was actually improved after starting their own businesses. Approximately 50 percent of the respondents believed that starting own business had no effect on their marriage. We did not have any information if these couples were working together in business, and these assessments were only based on entrepreneurs' own perceptions. Their spouses may or may not agree with the assessment of new venture creation on their marriage, and we did not ask spouses to respond.

Table 12—Effect on Marriage		
	Rural	**Urban**
Improved	20.1%	22.3%
No Effect	49.2%	50.9%
Some Problems	22.1%	17.7%
Estranged	1.5%	1.5%
Separated	.5%	1.1%
Divorced	6.5%	6.4%
Total	100.0%	100.0%
N	199	265
Chi Square	0.856	
Gamma	0.409	
Note: * significant at 0.1, ** significant at 0.01, *** significant at 0.001		

Discussion and Implications

Entrepreneurship has been mystified by scholars in many ways. Whether it is a micro approach or a macro approach, entrepreneurs have been studied and categorized as key drivers with respect to social movement, economic development, and ecological transformation. One thing we have not discussed much relates to community settings of entrepreneurial activities—rural versus urban. Sociology scholars introduced different theories to explain how urban and rural people connect with others (Amato, 1993) based on social disorganization perspective, environmental overload, and subcultural theory. These various aspects support many assumptions that (1) urban entrepreneurs have more exposure to entrepreneurial spirit, opportunities, resources, networks, capital, and support systems; (2) urban entrepreneurs have the advantage to gain experiences and skills that are offered by a boarder spectrum of educational institutions, training facilities, service organizations, and other infrastructure, and (3) urban entrepreneurs and their families have more access to a wide variety of services that will improve/enhance personal and family well-being, such as healthcare, retirement, and insurance programs.

Our study was designed to explore the differences between urban and rural entrepreneurs with respect to demographics, business profile, entrepreneurial characteristics, expectations, and outcome associated with new venture creation. More than 500 entrepreneurs in the Northern Delta region responded to our survey, and the results showed interesting comparisons between urban and rural entrepreneurs. In general, most respondents were male, white, and between 30 and 50 years of age. More urban entrepreneurs had some college or higher education, and more rural entrepreneurs were married with children. As we discussed earlier that urban entrepreneurs would have more access to education and skill training programs. Rural communities often maintain stronger family value and cultural heritage; therefore it is reasonable to expect more rural entrepreneurs to be married with children.

Our survey results mirrored the findings in entrepreneurship literature—both rural and urban entrepreneurs have characteristics of independence, control, creativity, and risks acceptance. Interestingly approximately 1/3 of our respondents did not have any line experience prior to starting own business. Only 1/2 respondents had some operation experience and management experience prior to starting own business. Literature discussed several reasons of failure in new venture creation, and lack of experiences is one of the key elements (Liang & Dunn, 2013).

Urban respondents were more likely to be optimistic than rural respondents in our survey. Urban respondents were also more likely to be realistic than rural respondents. More urban respondents expected to be happier and financially better off, while rural respondents were more conservative in assessing their expectations in new venture creation process. There were no significant differences between rural

entrepreneurs and urban entrepreneurs when evaluating the outcome of new venture creation—most of them believed that their businesses were up and running well, the sales and profit were about the same as expected, and their estimated annual sales were less than $500,000. The lessons learned were also similar between rural and urban entrepreneurs starting own business was harder than expected, and starting a business took more time than expected. Even with all the challenges and hard work, majority respondents still revealed positive experiences from—starting and running own businesses. They also believed that their family situations were better off, and their family would support them to start another new venture in the future.

Despite such positive assessment and self-satisfaction, many respondents in our survey were candid about some impacts on their marriage due to starting and running own businesses. Fifty percent of respondents in our survey said that the new venture creation had no impacts on their marriage. About 20 percent respondents agreed that their marriage was improved after starting the business. The rest of respondents had some problems with their spouses. It is not clear to us whether the marital issues existed prior to or after the new venture creation process. Scholars in psychology and entrepreneurship have presented both sides of the arguments. Some support that new venture creation actually enhances couple's working relationship and family value. The counter arguments indicating that mixing working relationship with marriage will create barriers and gaps in couple's romance and communication. In our case, there are really no significant differences between rural and urban entrepreneurs with respect to marital issues and new venture creation.

More public policies emphasize encouraging and promoting rural economic development by stimulating entrepreneurial activities. Rural communities indeed face different challenges and constraints comparing to urban communities. Accessibility, affordability, availability, and accountability associated with education, healthcare, capital, employment, and information become essential to incentivize rural entrepreneurship. Entrepreneurs are entrepreneurs, and their spirit and characteristics are much the same no matter where they reside. Successful policies need to provide resources and support to rural entrepreneurs to establish a strong and sustainable framework for rural economic development that will reduce financial burdens and investment risks. Public policies could also be established to enhance cultural recognition and environmental advantage for rural entrepreneurs where values of heritage and family are critical for prosperity.

References

Aldrich, H. E. & Cliff, J. E. (2003). The pervasive effects of family on entrepreneurship: Towards a family embeddedness perspective. *Journal of Business Venturing, 18,* 573–596.

Allen, K. (1995). *Launching new ventures an entrepreneurial approach.* Chicago, Upstart Publishing Company.

Amato, P. (1993). Urban-rural differences in helping friends and family members. *Social Psychology Quarterly, 56* (4), 249–262.

Ardichhvili, A., Cardozo, R., & Ray, S. (1993). A theory of entrepreneurial opportunity identification and development. *Journal of Business Venturing, 18* (1), 105–123.

Baron, R. & Shane. S. (2005). *Entrepreneurship: A process perspective,* 1st Edition, Mason, Ohio, South-Western Publishing, p. 60.

Brocas, I., & Carrillo, J. (2004). Entrepreneurial boldness and excessive investment. *Journal of Economics & Management Strategy, 13* (2), Summer, 322.

Bruce, D. (1999). Do husbands matter? Married women entering self-employment. *Small Business Economics, 13,* 317–29.

Bures, A. L. et al. (Winter 1995–1996). The effects of spousal support and gender on worker's stress and job satisfaction: A cross national investigation of dual career couples. *Journal of Applied Business Research, 12* (1), 52–58.

Burke, K., Czech, D. R., Knight, J. L., Scott, L. A., Joyner, A. B., Benton, S. G., & Roughton, H. K. (2006), An exploratory investigation of superstition, personal control, optimism and pessimism in NCAA Division I intercollegiate student-athletes. The *On-line Journal of Sport Psychology,* http://www/athleticinsight.com/vol8iss2/superstition.htm

Burke, K., Joyner, A. B., Czech, D. R., & Wilson, M. J. (2000). An investigation of concurrent validity between two optimism/pessimism questionnaires: The Life Orientation Test-Revised and the Optimism/Pessimism Scale. *Current Psychology, 19* (2), 129–136.

Centre for Confidence and Well-being (2006). *Positive Psychology Resource, Optimism.* http://www.centreforconfidence.co.uk/pp/index.php?p=c21kPTQ=

Chang, E. (2001. Introduction: Optimism and pessimism and moving beyond the most fundamental question. *Optimism and Pessimism,* Washington, D.C. American Psychological Association. p. 5.

Coelho, M., & De Meza, D. (2006). Self deception, self selection, self destruction: An experimental investigation of adverse selection. London School of Economics, http://cebr.dk/upload/demeza-001.pdf

Crane, F., & Crane, E. C. (2007). Dispositional optimism and entrepreneurial success. *The Psychologist-Manager Journal, 10* (1), 23.

Crane, F., & Sohl, J. (2004). Imperatives to venture success. *International Journal of Entrepreneurship and Innovation, 5* (2), 99.

Creed, P., Patton, W., & Bartrum, D. (2002). Multidimensional properties of the LOT-R: Effects of optimism and pessimism on career and well-being related variables in adolescents. *Journal of Career Assessment, 10* (1), 42–61.

Day, L., & Maltby, J. (2003). Belief in good luck and psychological well-being: The mediating role of optimism and irrational beliefs. *The Journal of Psychology, 137* (1), 108.

De Meza, D., & Southey, C. (1996). The borrower's curse: Optimism, finance and entrepreneurship. *The Economic Journal, 106,* March, 385.

Fraser, S., & Greene, F. J. (2006). The effects of experience on entrepreneurial optimism and uncertainty. *Economica, 73,* 169–192.

Haugen, R., Ommundsen, Y., & Lund, T. (2004). The concept of expectancy: A central factor in various personality dispositions. *Educational Psychology, 24* (1), 53.

Hey, J. (1984). The economics of optimism and pessimism. *KTKLOS, 37* (2). University of York, England, p. 204.

Hmieleski, K., & Baron, R. (2009). Entrepreneurs' optimism and new venture performance: A social cognitive perspective, *Academy of Management Journal, 52* (3), 473–488.

Jackson, T., Weiss, K., Lundquist, J., & Soderlind, A. (2002). Perceptions of goal-directed activities of optimists and pessimists: A personal projects analysis. *The Journal of Psychology, 136* (5), 528.

King, C. A. (1998). Family-owned firms need planners' help in designing pay. *National Underwriter Life & Health, 102* (43), October 26, 53–54.

Kuratko, D., & Hodgetts, R. (2004). *Entrepreneurship,* 5th Edition, Mason Ohio, South-Western, p. 111.

Leung, B. W., Moneta, G., & McBrice-Chang, C. (2005). Think positively: Optimism and life satisfaction in late life. *Journal of Aging & Human Development, 61* (4), 335.

Liang, K., & Dunn, P. (2003). Love, life, and family ties: Couples' assessment of new venture creation and business development and family relationships. *Proceedings of the Association for Small Business and Entrepreneurship.* http://www.sbaer.uca.edu/research/asbe/2003/pdfs/hub/24Liang&.pdf

Liang, K., & Dunn, P. (2008). Are entrepreneurs optimistic, realistic, both or fuzzy? *Academy of Entrepreneurship, 14* (1 & 2), 51–76.

Liang, C., & Dunn, P. (2011). Satisfaction or business savvy—Examining the outcome of new venture creation with respect to entrepreneurial characteristics, expectation, optimism, realism, and pessimism. *Academy of Entrepreneurship, 17* (2), 97–116.

Liang, C., & Dunn, P. (2012). Entrepreneurial learning and business assessment—What new decisions would be made after learning? *Journal of Business and Entrepreneurship, 24* (1), 105–122.

Liang, C. & Dunn, P. (2013) "The love of my life" or "The life I love"—Investigating impacts of new venture creation on marriage. *Journal of Business and Entrepreneurship, 5,* 95–114.

Lieberman, S. (2000). All in the family. *Restaurant Hospitality LXXXIV,* March, 24.

Litt, M. D., Tennen, H., Aftleck, G., & Klock, S. (1992). Coping and cognitive factors in adaptation to in vitro fertilization failure. *Journal of Behavioral Medicine, 15,* 171–187.

Malach-Pines, A., Sadeh, A., Dvir, D., & Yafe-Yanai, 0. (2002). Entrepreneurs and managers: Similar yet different. *The International Journal of Organizational Analysis, 10* (2), 174.

Manove, M. (2000). Entrepreneurs, optimism and the competitive edge. Boston University and CEMFI, http://www.bu.edu/econ/faculty/manove/Opt.pdf

McColl-Kennedy, J. R., & Anderson, R. D. (2005). Subordinate-manager gender combination and perceived leadership style influence on emotions, self-esteem and organizational commitment. *Journal of Business Research, 58* (2), 115.

Perczek, R., Carver, C., Price, A., & Pozo-Kaderman, C. (2000). Coping, mood, and aspects of personality in Spanish translation and evidence of convergence with English versions. *Journal of Personality Assessment, 74* (1), 63–87.

Petrakis, P. E. (2005). Risk perception, risk propensity and entrepreneurial behavior: The Greek case. *The Journal of American Academy of Business, 7* (1), September, Cambridge, 237.

Puri, M., & Robinson, D. T. (2004). Optimism, work/life choices, and entrepreneurship. http://www.worldbank.org/finance/assets/images/manju_puri_entrepreneurship_dr_3.pdf

Puskar, K. R., Sereika, S. M., Lamb, J., Tusaie-Mumford, K., & Mcguinness, T. (1999). Optimism and its relationship to depression. *Coping, Anger, and Life Events in Rural Adolescents, 20* (2), 115–130.

Sarasvathy, S. (2003). The questions we ask and the questions we care about: Reformulating some problems in entrepreneurship research. *Journal of Business Venturing, 19* (6), 707–717.

Scheier, M. F., & Carver, C. S. (1987). Dispositional optimism and physical well-being: The influence of generalized outcome expectancies on health. *Journal of Personality, 55* (2), 188.

Seligman, M. E. P., & Schulman, P. (1986). Explanatory style as a predictor of productivity and quitting amongst life insurance sales agents. *Journal of Personality and Social Psychology, 50,* 832–838.

Shane, S., & Venkataraman, S. (2000). The promise of entrepreneurship as a field of research. *The Academy of Management Review, 25* (1), 217–226.

Simon, M., & Houghton, S. (2002). The relationship among biases, misperceptions, and the introduction of pioneering products: Examining differences in venture decision contexts. *Entrepreneurship Theory and Practice,* Winter, Baylor University, 118.

Sujan, H. (1999). Optimism and street smarts: Identifying and improving salesperson intelligence. *Journal of Personal Selling & Sales Management, 19* (3), 26.

Sydney, E., Hadley, W., Allen, D. N., Palmer, S., Klosky, J., Deptula, D., Thomas, J., & Cohen, R. (2005). A new measure of children's optimism and pessimism: The youth life orientation test. *Journal of Child Psychology and Psychiatry, 46* (5), 548.

Walker, B. L., Nail, L. M., Larsen, L., Magill, J., & Schwartz, A. (1996). Concerns, affect, and cognitive disruption following completion of radiation treatment for localized breast or prostate cancer. *Oncol Nurs Forum, 23* (8), 1181–1187.

Wrosch, C., & Scheier, M. (2003). Personality and quality of life: The importance of optimism and goal adjustment. *Quality of Life Research* 12 (Suppl. 1) Kluwer Academic Publishers, Netherlands p 64, 69.